Audio for Games

Planning, Process, and Production

Alexander Brandon

New Riders

NRG

New Riders Games
New Riders
1249 Eighth Street • Berkeley, CA 94710

Audio for Games: Planning, Process, and Production
Alexander Brandon
Copyright © 2005 by Alexander Brandon

Published by New Riders. For information on New Riders Games books, contact:

New Riders
1249 Eighth Street
Berkeley, CA 94710
(510) 524-2178
Fax: (510) 524-2221
http://www.peachpit.com
To report errors, please send a note to errata@peachpit.com
New Riders is an imprint of Peachpit, a division of Pearson Education

Editor: Jacqueline Aaron
Production Editor: Lisa Brazieal
Project Editor: Wendy Sharp
Technical Editor: Guy Whitmore
Copy Editor: Hon Walker
Interior design: Frances Baca
Compositor: Owen Wolfson
Indexer: Julie Bess
Cover design: Aren Howell
Cover photo: Veer

ISBN 0-7357-1413-4
9 8 7 6 5 4 3 2 1
Printed and bound in the United States of America

This book is dedicated to Jeanette, Nicholas, Joel,
Cynthia, Mark, Kathy, and the quest for a better way…

Acknowledgements

Without these people, this book would have not been possible… while such a statement is commonplace as the preface to most literature, in this case I can't stress its truth strongly enough.

First, thanks go to George Sanger, who very graciously showed me the path to authorship. To Stephanie Wall for her enthusiasm with all things in the game industry and initiating this project. To Guy Whitmore, for his excellent technical editing and very astute comments. To Jacqueline Aaron, the most patient, kind and professional editor I could ask for. To Hon Walker for his complete and focused finishing touches. To Wendy Sharp, who like Jacqueline showed unparalleled patience and understanding as the book's editor. To Lisa Brazieal and Owen Wolfson for magically turning my boring Word documents into something very polished. To Mimi Heft for her great help with illustrations. To Dave Maldonado for taking time out of his busy schedule to create the menacing "Sentinoid" (found in Chapter 8).

Hirokazu Tanaka was the first video game music composer to inspire me. I wouldn't be in my profession if it wasn't for Tanaka-san's work. My colleagues in the industry are also strong supports in the ladder of my experience with video games. There are far too many to list, but I thank them all.

Contents At a Glance

Table of Contents

Introduction

ALL OF US in the game development community know that game audio has grown considerably in the last 20 years. After roughly one-fifth the length of time that movies and television have taken to evolve, videogames are now starting to be held to the same high standards for quality. It was one thing to have a game magazine say, "This game's soundtrack would be right at home in a film," but now that the same is being said by general-interest publications like *Newsweek* and *Entertainment Weekly,* it's clear that even the harshest critics are beginning to acknowledge the excellence of audio in games.

The game industry has exploded in the past five years, thus raising the bar on game audio quality. Now anyone who can write music and create sound can have his or her work included in a game, and in fact there is usually competition to do so. Game-audio veterans who once spent their time tweaking lines of code and writing text files to create sound and music are now obsolete, replaced by teams of savvy studio composers and sound designers with their own custom and much more user-friendly integration tools.

For the paranoid geek who grew up living and breathing the smaller, more aesthetically driven, closer-knit community of videogame development, this recent development is seen as an intrusion, a threat to what once was a small and vibrantly artistic form of entertainment. That is true, but I think the advantages outweigh the threat. Where once we were limited by memory registers and minuscule file sizes, we now can use everything from the grandest orchestra to the most advanced synthesizer as our instruments. We have the same tools the Grammy winners do. If we could create joy and pain from simple FM synthesis, imagine what we can achieve now.

With all this change, a key point to remember is that just because you can write music and create sound effects doesn't mean you can make them sound good—or, more importantly, make them sound good in a game. Simply put, it's a new kind of challenge.

Most of this challenge is evident in the adaptive nature of audio for games. These days, the score in a game doesn't have to sound the same each time the game is played. Music can follow action, or a lack of action, dynamically. Also, now when a game's objects bounce, crash, slide, or touch each other in different ways, hundreds of sounds—instead of just one, as in the old days—are being combined to simulate reality more effectively. Such capabilities are huge, but they are perhaps the most difficult of all to achieve successfully.

I was fortunate enough to have been born between the geeks and the savvy composers. I have an unusually deep respect for our beloved game industry's past and a clear and focused eye on its future. It is this unique perspective that has formed the foundation for *Audio for Games: Planning, Process, and Production,* which is meant to tackle the new challenge of creating compelling and unique content in the world of game audio.

Rising to the Challenge

Producing game audio once meant writing a few pieces of music, creating 30 or so sound effects, and hard-coding them. Having more than one person involved was unheard-of. Now a typical high-profile title contains thousands of sound effects, tens of thousands of lines of dialogue, and at least an hour of music, with up to a dozen people providing and integrating the content.

Postproduction and mastering are now common, and the advent of such effects as the physics system mentioned earlier and real-time reverb in conjunction with multichannel surround is making game audio more and more similar to the most effective moments you'll experience in a movie theater.

What some people tend to find boring about game audio development is something we will cover in detail: The same organizational issues that plague small and medium-size businesses affect game teams, and proper management with communication and coordination is vital.

In this book I intend not only to highlight skills and techniques important to the game-audio development process, but also to explain just what techniques will be making games an independent form of entertainment, with their audio—dare I say it?—more effective than that of film.

Wake-up Call to Developers

A couple of years ago I had the opportunity to interview a fairly well-known film composer who worked for a prestigious music production house. The production house supplies at least a third of the soundtracks for major motion pictures. The composer had recently completed his first soundtrack for a major game title, and needless to say I was excited at the prospect of the film world joining hands with the game industry. Hollywood, with all its glamour and fame, had turned an interested eye in our direction—what a monumental step!

I called up the production house and surprisingly enough was transferred directly to the composer. I was nervous as he picked up the phone. The words fell out of my mouth: "Hello! I'm doing an article about film composers in the game industry, and I have to say you're the first major film composer to have scored a game … and … and …" Before I could embarrass myself any further, I decided to dive right in. "How did it feel to work on a game?"

His answers were quick, polite, and informative. They were also a bit shocking. "I enjoyed it. But, you see, I don't do this sort of thing usually. I write music for films," he began.

I thought to myself, *Yes, indeed you do; I'm aware of that.* He continued as my jaw dropped to the floor. "The last game I played, I think, was *Pong* in 1978. I really don't play games. Believe me, I was fascinated with how my cues were being used and the process behind it all, but I really don't do this sort of thing normally."

The conversation continued: it was an interesting wake-up call. For the first time in my experience, production was separated from implementation by thousands of miles. The esteemed composer in California simply received screen shots and communications from developers in Japan; the developers described the scenes and situations; and then the composer wrote the score.

It was then up to me to ask myself those moral questions that often infuriate the purist and satisfy the market-milker. Was this process right? Was it a good thing to do? Well, those are tough ones. Let's make it easier by asking, Was it effective? Until now, game composers wrote for games, and movie composers wrote for movies. Today the field is more diverse, more specialized. Production and implementation are separate, giving the "one-man show" audio teams less responsibility and, some say, less power.

The movie industry, and even more so the flailing music industry, is seeing games as a major opportunity. *NBA Live* included a soundtrack and is reported to be the first game soundtrack to have gone platinum, since the title sold more than a million copies. The old-school, hardcore game-sound engineers and composers are a dying breed. Just what can a guy in his bedroom do with two PCs, a DAT recorder, and a few pieces of MIDI gear to compete with million-dollar production houses and mighty record companies with far more resources and marketing savvy? Plenty. There is also a lot that those million dollar studios can't do in games. That's what this book is about: bringing the old school into the present and giving the newcomers from the game community as well as from Hollywood the information they need to become interactive-audio experts.

Read on. Welcome to the new world.

CHAPTER 1

A Development Process Map of Game-Audio Implementation

THE DIAGRAM on the following pages lays out the subject of this chapter: the *development process map* (DPM) for preproduction (**Figure 1.1**) and production (**Figure 1.2**). This visual model is used to guide the game development process for audio preproduction and production. In this chapter I will describe each of the elements of the DPM using a sample project.

Preproduction

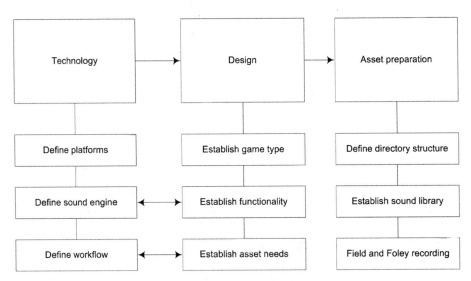

FIGURE 1.1 Creating a development process map (DPM) for your audio preproduction will make it easier to track game-related elements such as technology, design, and the preparation of assets.

Production

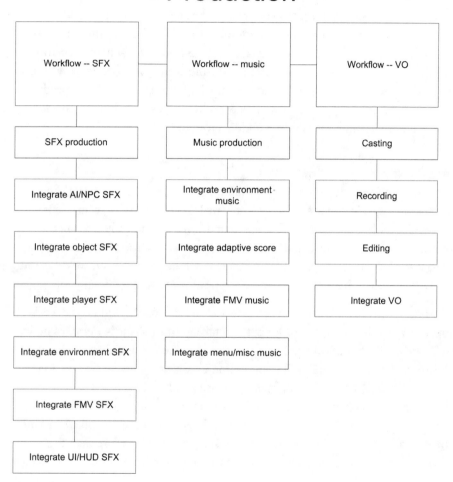

FIGURE 1.2 For audio production, as with preproduction, a DPM gives you a visual overview of your development cycle that includes as many levels of detail as you need.

Development Process

Let's begin with something most production-oriented folks take for granted: planning. The desire to jump in and write songs, create incredible sounds, incorporate the latest middleware surround-sound solution, and hire the latest superstar actor for voice-over work makes us grind our teeth with anticipation, but it can lead to a mountain of wasted work and plenty of raised voices if it isn't planned properly. On the other hand, too much planning can lead to a product that is never released—and that, well, raises other voices. Let's look at how following the DPM can help us find a middle ground.

Why Do You Need a DPM?

Three factors determine the success or failure of any project: whether it's released on time, how closely it meets its budget, how well the product sells (its marketing, its appeal, and the fun factor). So a studio that doesn't want its project to fail must follow a schedule, a budget, and a plan. And audio isn't something thrown in at the last second anymore. We can't get away with a few cute beeps if we expect to satisfy the public. Therefore we plan, we communicate, and we document.

All of my discussions in this chapter have an eye toward who will do the work, how much it will cost, and how long it will take to finish. This is weird, I know: We're artists, not programmers, and God knows we're not accountants. How can we expect to plan while still maintaining a passion for artistic expression? Simple answer: Follow a development process map. I don't care if you want to write music while sitting in a cramped bedroom studio or lead a staff at a huge in-house production facility with an office as large as Michael Douglas's in *Wall Street*. Granted, the audio lead will want to keep track of far more than the sound effects engineer will, but if you don't have a process in place, you won't get your project done.

Knuckle down with this now, and you'll save yourself a boatload of composition and sound-design time later. Having said that, I'm not deluded. We *are* game designers. Our lives are devoted to enjoying ourselves and making things as easy as possible. Since I know this as well as anyone, I'm not going to give you a dismally boring book of nothing but text and charts and graphs. We're going to have fun. On to making game audio!

What Is a DPM?

This chapter represents an effort to define an overall effective and streamlined way to add sound to a game. The following pages explain the DPM in the context of a typical game project. The game type I use as an example is a role-playing game (RPG), but this chapter applies to other types of games as well—sports, action, puzzle, and so on.

What is a DPM? It's fairly self-explanatory: a picture of your development cycle. A DPM makes your life easier by eliminating quite a few of those exhaustive sound-design document pages, compressing them into a big map that can have as many layers of detail as you wish. Companies use maps (business activity maps, or BAMs) to outline their functions. The DPM I'm using is rather generic but can be applied to the development of any game. These maps are like gold when they're used properly—they're easy to start, not too tough to finish, and worth the effort.

> **NOTE** A DPM is most helpful when it's used as more than simply a flow-chart. A flowchart shows a process, but not who will do the work or how the work will be done. A DPM, though, lets you add levels of detail, embedding them so as not to create too cluttered a document. Use hyperlinks or book-marks so that clicking any one item displays a description along with other relevant data. Some companies have released software costing tens of thou-sands of dollars that let you accomplish this, but it can be done just as eas-ily by writing some HTML code or using Microsoft Frontpage or Macromedia Dreamweaver. I used Microsoft Visio to create Figures 1.1 and 1.2.

As you can see, the DPM covered in this chapter has two major sections: pre-production and production. You may wonder why postproduction is missing. At most game companies these days, games don't have a postproduction cycle, espe-cially for audio. Bizarre, considering that films have a postproduction cycle, but that cycle is far more clear-cut for films than for games: You can finish shooting, edit the film, and send it off to the composer. Most games, on the other hand, are tweaked in some form or another right up until their ship date.

Preproduction

Now that we've come to grips with what a DPM is and why you need one, let's examine what it entails.

Technology

Although many processes are linear in nature, including the writing of this book and the act of reading it, we need to remember that some aspects of design as well as technology are best worked on simultaneously, at the beginning of a game project. In an ideal world, a game's design would be complete before any of the technology was developed, but the game industry is a business, and multi-tasking isn't just an exciting capability of a 1980s operating system anymore.

The first factor to consider is your audience. You need to know what platforms you'll be working on before you can do anything else. Believe it or not, the major publishers like Sony and Nintendo really do try to market their platform to specific groups. Nintendo has always had a stranglehold on younger players, and Sony has been providing first-generation players with many more titles oriented toward adults and young adults. Those and other marketing considerations are good to keep in mind when thinking about the audio for your title, because they identify your audience.

Defining the platform

For our example, we'll pick the most popular platform at the time of this writing, Sony's PlayStation 2. With more than 60 million units sold, it's the world heavyweight champion of game consoles.

If you're reading this in 2015 and are thinking you're wasting your time, stop! If I mention 2 MB of memory and you have 32 MB, just swap the figures. The DPM will still work fine, no matter what your architecture is.

Defining the sound engine

Now that we've defined our platform, we can start to define our sound engine. (For more details on the sound engine, see Chapter 3, "Technology"; we'll discuss multiplatform development in that chapter as well.) Glance back at the preproduction DPM (**Figure 1.1**), and notice that "Define sound engine" ties in with "Establish functionality." This is where we begin to see that the nature of our

DPM is to establish dependencies and the use of systems, rather than to exist as a simplified linear workflow. You can't define a sound engine unless you first know what your platform is and what kind of game you're making. Take a look at **Figure 1.3**.

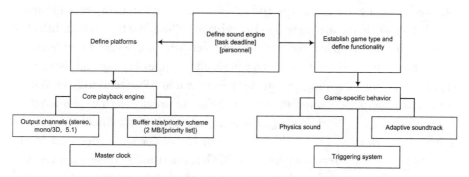

FIGURE 1.3 Relationships within the development process map (DPM) let you define the sound engine in detail.

We've increased the level of detail for the task of defining the sound engine, which now lists the deadline and the person who will be working on the task. Remember, you can keep adding as many levels of detail as you want. When your platform is defined, you can establish a *core playback engine,* which will vary depending on the application programming interface (API) that directly inter-acts with the hardware of the platform. Simply put, the programming team will use the core playback engine as a template for their work. Once you've defined your game's design and functionality, you can plan its game-specific behavior.

Defining the core playback engine

The core playback engine essentially comprises the cylinder block of the sound engine. It is what determines whether your game audio will be in stereo or 5.1 channels, or both. It determines how many sounds you can play at once, as well as how many pieces of music. It also handles any hardware issues specific to a platform. For example, if the platform featured real-time DTS surround-sound encoding and decoding, the core playback engine would possess the instructions to funnel the sounds through that chip or chip set. Sometimes, in order to keep sounds timed to events properly, a master clock is used. The clock can also sync two streams together so that if one stops and is triggered again, it can begin at the correct time subdivision. A core playback engine can be applied to any game type, but unless you're familiar with the platform you're developing on, you're not going to have this engine.

Establishing game type and defining functionality

We need to define our game type and establish game functionality on a minimal level before we define the game-specific behavior. The game type is established by the high-level creative directors and producers within a development team or company, and it will differ based on the kind of games these groups have expertise in. When deciding on a game type, note that RPGs tend to have more complexity, and players who can tackle an RPG can usually learn to play a fighting game (such as *Mortal Kombat*), a sports game (such as the *Madden* series), or a first-person shooter (FPS, such as *Doom 3* or *Halo*). The same goes for a development team—if the team can create an RPG, it can usually create other game types with relative ease, though there are many considerations to each game type. Think of it in terms of a piano player who learns to play classical and jazz first. After that, other styles are easier to learn, as opposed to approaching other styles first and then attempting classical or jazz.

Defining game-specific behavior

Once our game type and initial functionality have been established, we can go on to define our game-specific behavior. Game-specific behavior comprises everything outside of the core engine running the sound. For example, will the main character have the ability to jump and shout a horrific battle cry at the same time? When players push a button in the user interface, will they hear a bleep or a cheesy "Good job"? Will objects bounce around when thrown and make realistic noises upon impact? Will your music go from suspenseful to lilting and back again depending on what the player does? All of these questions are answered by game-specific behavior. Defining this behavior isn't easy.

It's important to keep in mind that because functionality is linked to game design, the design will change throughout the development cycle. Therefore, it's impossible to be 100 percent sure that a game-specific behavior is permanent when it's written down initially. To combat this uncertainty, we define our behavior in iterations. First, we generalize. Using an RPG as our example, we can make some assumptions before we even see a game design document: The game will have player characters (aka PCs, characters in the game that the person playing the game can control) and nonplayer characters (NPCs, characters in the game that characters do not control). Chances are they'll all have feet, even if they don't walk on legs. The fact that our characters have feet has already led us to deduce that we will need footstep sounds and some sort of randomization code to keep them from being repetitive. We might even want to separate the heel and toe sounds so that when any character runs, whether PC or NPC, we can save memory by making the sounds play closer together and faster.

How does a game's type affect decisions like these? Game-specific behavior for a sports game, for example, will differ greatly from that of an RPG. In a football game, the playing field is the only location, and while there might be different stadium or field selections, having this limitation enables more work to be done on character complexity (such as a quarterback and the kind of passes and plays he can accomplish), since less needs to be done on the environment. Therefore, whoever is handling audio would need to consider those differences when undertaking the project, because creating character sounds and creating environmental sounds are different skills.

Dependencies

We haven't yet seen a single demo or piece of artwork, but we've already established a basic system to add to our game-specific behavior. This doesn't mean that you sound guys will stop whining—you still have *dependencies*. Keep that important word in mind, because dependencies are what you rely on to complete work to the whole team's liking, not just yours. For example, if you need to create a sound for a shotgun but aren't sure exactly how it will be animated, the need for an animation to look at is a dependency. When you have a deadline for certain sounds or music to be delivered, that too is a dependency. Now that we've established what a dependency is, let's take a look at how we deal with them.

Illustrative Examples of Early Audio Meetings

During development, it becomes all too easy to forget about communication between developers. Yes, we have a DPM, and we've identified work that needs to be done, but does that mean we can communicate it to those who need to be aware of it? The following examples will help you understand what can happen as a result of bad communication and what can happen as a result of good communication.

Although half fiction and half fact, this type of conversation has happened to most of us at least once. Bless the gaming world's slow but sure approach to maturity, because this meeting is becoming more of a rarity—but forms of it still happen everywhere.

Someone standing surreptitiously in the shadowy corner of the conference room takes the meeting minutes. At the table sit the project director, the lead designer, the audio director, the lead programmer, the producer, and the associate producer. A hush falls over the group as the meeting begins.

Audio director: Welcome, everyone. I'd like to begin by getting an idea of what our schedule and budget are so we can at least set our end goals in place.

Producer: Neither is final.

(*Long pause.*)

Audio director: Er … OK. In that case, at least we know we're working on an RPG. I'd like to continue by asking the project director and lead designer if they have any specific ideas about what they'd like to see in this product audiowise that hasn't been done before, or that could be improved from previous projects.

(*Project director and lead designer look at one another, then turn back and shrug.*)

Project director: Nothing really; let's just at least make the audio as good as the last game I worked on. I think if we set the bar there, it'll still be higher than other games out there.

CONTINUED ▶

Illustrative Examples of Early Audio Meetings, continued...

Lead designer: Yeah, essentially what he said. I don't want too much music. I also don't want it to be obtrusive. I want it to be supersubtle.

Audio director: Good, excellent. (*Scribbles in notepad.*) At this point we'll be starting to create our sound lists so that you can see what we'll be working on, and once a month I'd like to schedule a meeting where we can make sure that the audio team is on track.

Producer: When?

Audio director: When would work best? First Friday of every month? 3 p.m.?

Producer: Won't work. I'll get back to you.

Audio director: No problem. (*Turns to lead programmer.*) I have a simplified set of specs for our audio engine, and ...

Lead programmer: We're using the one that came with the engine we licensed.

Audio director (*ruffled, but regaining composure*): OK, I haven't had a chance to review it, thanks for the info. I'll take a look, and once the sound programmer ...

Lead programmer: Sound programmer?

Audio director: Well, aren't we going to ...

Lead programmer: We'll use Phil for a couple of months if you have anything you need done.

Audio director: I think that it'll probably take more than a couple of months considering our scope, since the basic design seems to indicate ...

Associate producer: It damn well better not!

Project director: OK, we need to discuss these issues separately. Anything else?

CONTINUED ▶

Illustrative Examples of Early Audio Meetings, continued...

Audio director: Maybe if we just …

Lead designer: Just make some cool samples for us. We're not far enough along to implement anything.

Project director: Good plan.

Producer: I think we're done.

(*The scene fades and we adjourn to another meeting, six months later. The mood is anxious.*)

Project director: We've got a problem here. We need audio.

Audio director: We're just now at a point where we can begin to …

Producer: Audio is lagging behind. What's the problem?

Audio director: OK. I've asked for project schedule cooperation for milestone dates and gotten absolutely no response. I've asked for art lists and gotten incomprehensible Excel spreadsheets in 4-point type. I've asked for programmer support and gotten estimates for the start of work on the sound engine, right up until last week, when we started debugging the damn thing and are still knee-deep in crashes. How's that for a problem?

Producer: Well, audio really needs to buckle down.

Audio director: Buckle *this*, you (*expletives deleted*).

Now, these meeting examples are exaggerated, but for many meetings, the essence of what is communicated is dead-on. Let's continue with what this meeting *should have* sounded like. The same players are at the table.

Audio director: Hello, everybody. Thanks for coming.

Project director: Why don't I start?

CONTINUED ▶

Illustrative Examples of Early Audio Meetings, continued...

Audio director: By all means.

Project director: I want your schedule and design doc in line with those of the other team leads. Our producer here will give you an example of how we do our schedules and design docs, and you can get initial versions to us next week. Oh, and I'll supply you with your budget by then as well.

Producer: I'll get this stuff to you today and go over it with you.

Audio director (*lip quivering while writing furiously*): Absolutely. (*Pauses for breath.*) Thanks, I'll get right on it. Now, in terms of technology …

Lead programmer: I'd like to have a meeting tomorrow about that.

Audio director: Great! (*Scribbles again.*) I'd like the lead designer and project director as well as you there so we can identify some basic but expandable functionality for the sound engine.

Lead programmer: No problem.

Lead designer: Sounds good. I have some specific ideas I'd like your opinion on.

Audio director: Excellent. That's all I have for now.

Project director: Great, let's adjourn.

(*And we fade to black, fading back into the meeting six months later.*)

Audio director: Well, our engine is up and running, half of our sounds are complete, 25 percent of the music is done, and we're also at about 25 percent of the sounds and music already implemented.

Producer: We're still under budget and right on schedule.

Project director: Fantastic. The game is sounding great, but I have a few comments about sound x, music y, and voice placeholder z.

Lead designer: I concur, and I have additional comments a and b.

CONTINUED ▶

Illustrative Examples of Early Audio Meetings, continued...

Audio director (*scribbling*): I agree with x, y, and b. Here's why I think z and a might not be a good idea....

Project director: That makes sense. Don't worry about z, then.

Lead designer: a could still work if we do plan q; here's how....

Audio director: Hey, true. Good idea; let's try plan q with a and test the results Thursday. Make sure to check the bug database to track our changes to the game.

Lead designer: Sounds good.

Lead programmer: Remember to keep your sound designers and composers informed about the right way to fill out a bug report concerning the sound engine or the trigger script system. We've been getting some odd requests lately.

Audio director: You got it. Refer a couple to me and I'll have a meeting with my guys. I'll also make sure the process is documented in our design doc. Heads will roll if you get any more of this. (*Laughs.*)

Lead programmer: Thanks.

Producer: Oh, the marketing folks need some assets from you; they should get in touch with you today about that.

Audio director: OK.

Project director: I'm very pleased with how things are going. Let's keep up the good work!

Audio director (*leaping into the air*): I love what you do for me, Toyyyy-ota!!!

(*Quizzical looks from around the room.*)

Both of these scenarios have been dramatized rather freely, but it's a solid lesson in communication. If we apply lessons one learns in organization development, we can see that the differences are clear between the two sets of meetings. Let's identify what made the first meeting a bad one.

The Bad Meeting

To sum up, characteristics of the bad meeting include the following:

▶ No schedule or budget has been established, and because of this, audio is likely to be underbudgeted in the end. Imagine if a producer requested a killer, world-class orchestral score on a $5000 budget by the end of the month.

▶ There are no universal guidelines for management documentation such as schedules and design documents.

▶ Not everyone is in agreement on workflow and technology.

▶ The team is generally uncertain about how audio will be integrated with the rest of the project, which leads to a lack of interest in audio.

▶ The result is a breakdown in communication and a failure to produce.

The Good Meeting

In contrast, characteristics of the good meeting include the following:

▶ The meetings started early in the project cycle.

▶ The leads are all interested in their own focus as well as the focus of the team as a whole.

▶ The project director has a clear management strategy for production.

▶ The audio director is straightforward about disagreement on issues and open to compromise.

Defining workflow

As my esteemed colleague Tom White, head of the MIDI Manufacturers Association, asks all too often, Who will do the work? Add this question—How and when will they do the work?—and you've got a good foundation for the most important information to gather during the early days of your project.

Now, why discuss workflow in the context of technology? Good question. Workflow affects all aspects of the project, from audio to graphics; when creating audio, we want to associate workflow with technology first. The implementation of audio usually differs with each new title, because the technology of games changes much faster than does the technology used in creating the audio itself. Still, keep in mind that defining a workflow is relevant to any aspect of preproduction or production. Defining a workflow should start with the project leads, in a meeting similar to the "good" example we've just considered. Once the technology has been at least preliminarily defined, we can proceed to using that technology to establish the game-specific behavior we discussed earlier. The lead programmer and the audio director should figure out the most effective (speed + kick-ass = most effective) way to use the new sound engine to implement the game's audio. They should also decide on the best way to handle the interplay between the game's assets (more on that below) and the people doing the implementing. Let's break down this task (as shown in **Figure 1.4**); in doing so, you'll notice an uncanny similarity to the workflow of production. This is intentional. Oh yes, this is also where the magic happens.

Each category of sounds is identified, from user interface sound effects (SFX) to full-motion video (FMV) music. Each category indicates who will do the work; provides a link to a list of assets such as SFX, music, and voice-over (VO); and includes a link to a document describing how the work is done. Note that the header also contains a task deadline and a personnel list. The audio director and lead programmer should be included here; together they will establish how implementation will happen for each category. The audio director will be responsible for the asset list and the sound-design document.

Asset list? Sound-design document? What are those? This brings us to the design portion of our preproduction phase.

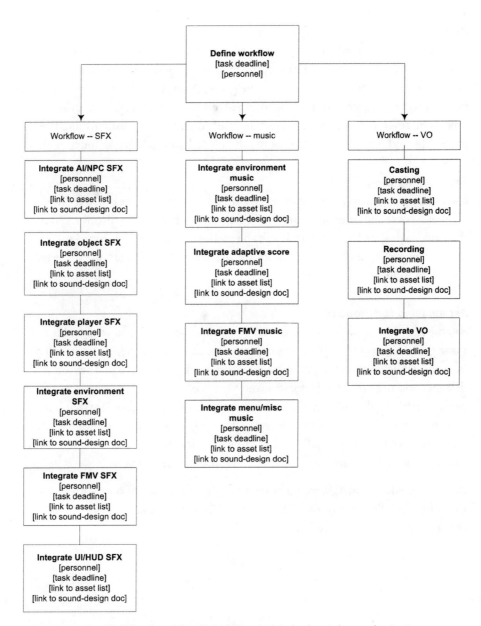

FIGURE 1.4 A well-defined workflow includes project tasks for each sound category.

Design

Game design, also known as *game mechanics* or *gameplay,* is similar to technology in how we link it to audio and how easily the work proceeds from start to finish. Game design is essentially the rules of the game. It defines what game type the product will be. Game design tends to be subject to more change than other aspects of development, and that affects sound. We'll begin by establishing the game type and moving on to the more difficult task of establishing functionality.

Establishing the game type

Establishing a game type is easy, since it isn't even your job unless you're the head of a company or game team in addition to being an audio director. Often the game type goes hand in hand with the platform it will be developed for, as I mentioned earlier in the chapter. Since we've already decided that our game type will be an RPG, let's continue.

Establishing functionality

Establishing functionality ties in closely with building our sound engine. It's a more difficult part of the planning process, as it includes the dependency-filled task of establishing asset needs. Who does this work, you may ask? The lead designer and the project director are your points of contact (sometimes just one or the other) for this information. They are the ones responsible for what happens onscreen. If an orc needs to attack with a club instead of a spear, for example, they would make that call. In the words of Tears for Fears, let's break it down again. **Figure 1.5** outlines the process of establishing functionality.

As we define functionality, we must keep in mind the limits of our platform, examine carefully what kinds of data we're dealing with, and then organize that data properly in a structured document.

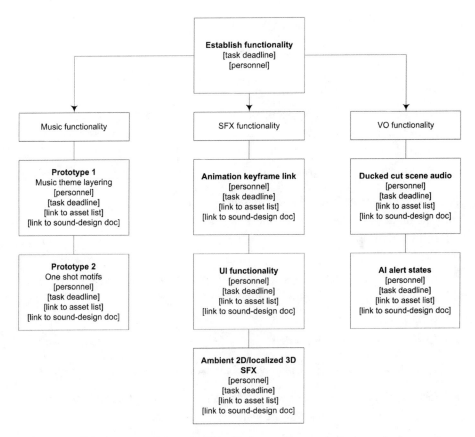

FIGURE 1.5 This document defines functionality for music, sound effects, and voice-overs.

A first draft of functionality for audio might be in the form of a feature set like this one:

SFX

▶   48 channels.

▶   Three-dimensional sound panned from the player.

▶   User interface mock-up with sounds listed.

Music

▶   Scripted one-shot (nonlooped) music playback for dramatic sequences.

▶   Layered music track that plays while a player is failing or succeeding in battle.

▶ Layered music track that plays when a nonplayer character enters the playing field.

Voice-over (VO)

▶ The NPC has x number of alert states for sound.

▶ Non-VO audio will duck (drop volume) by x decibels during a cut scene (a point in the game during which the player watches a video or an in-game scripted sequence and is not in control of onscreen events).

▶ The NPC will query various sound triggers.

This list will be located in the *sound-design document*, or SDD. It will integrate with the main game design document in such a way that each of these entries will be linked to something in the game design doc. For example, when you read "scripted one-shot music playback for dramatic sequences," you may wonder: What dramatic sequences? Click the sentence, and it will take you to the game design doc, where those dramatic sequences, which are known by many names, are listed. For example:

▶ In-game sequences/triggers/cut scenes

▶ Level 2, Meybourn Inn: The player triggers the bartender to raise the alarm.

▶ Level 2, Dismal Swamp: The player walks into the bog; the black dragon Stormbringer emerges from the water.

▶ And so on.

Each sequence should have a corresponding file or set of files, which are located in an *asset list* and are defined by the next step in our preproduction phase.

> **NOTE** If you have the time to budget, create prototypes. They can't be underestimated, especially for an adaptive soundtrack. Say someone suggests that a little theme plays when a nonplayer character comes onscreen. Cool idea, right? Well, it depends on how it's done. What kind of theme will it be? A few notes that repeat? A single instrument that plays varying notes? Great idea, but what the hell will it sound like? With a prototype you can answer these questions. Even if the game isn't ready for the audio to be implemented, you can still create a mock-up on the multitrack software (or hardware) of your choice and trigger it manually.

Establishing asset needs

The asset list must include absolutely every audio file that the game uses. This list should be controlled by only one person (usually the audio director) or at most two; if the audio director is also producing content, an associate director or even a sound designer can help keep it up-to-date. Although you can use a database, the asset list is best kept in the form of a spreadsheet because it lets you look at entire groups of sounds or music at once (see **Figure 1.6**).

	A	B	C	D	E	F	G
1		**Player SFX**					
2							
3	Description	Filename	Format	Audition	Filesize	Approved	Implemented
4	Knight Attack - Slash	KnightAttackSlash.wav	ADPCM	<click to hear file>	20k	Y	Y
5	Knight Attack - Stab	KnightAttackStab.wav	ADPCM	<click to hear file>	30k	Y	N
6	Knight Attack - Charge	KnightAttackCharge.wav	ADPCM	<click to hear file>	25k	N	N
7	Knight Footstep - Walk - Concrete1	FootstepKnightWalkConc1.wav	ADPCM	<click to hear file>	4k	Y	Y
8	Knight Footstep - Walk - Concrete2	FootstepKnightWalkConc2.wav	ADPCM	<click to hear file>	2k	Y	Y
9	Knight Footstep - Walk - Concrete3	FootstepKnightWalkConc3.wav	ADPCM	<click to hear file>	5k	Y	Y
10	Knight Footstep - Walk - Concrete4	FootstepKnightWalkConc4.wav	ADPCM	<click to hear file>	3k	Y	N
11	etc						
12							

FIGURE 1.6 Because an asset list includes vast amounts of information in groups, it exists best as a spreadsheet.

In **Figure 1.6**, you can see a fairly general-purpose asset list, with each entry detailing a sound's description, its filename and format, a way to preview (*audition*) it, its file size, whether it has been approved, and whether it has been implemented. An additional column for notes or comments is also useful.

If you're familiar with database and network code, you can program the links from the list to files for auditioning. You might be thinking that it'd be time-consuming to find the file sizes and enter the values by hand. Well, you're right. You'll need a programmer to help you link your asset list entries to the assets themselves.

Another time-saver a programmer can offer is including the filename for your assets in the sound diagnostic tools. We'll explore diagnostic tools more fully later, but you want this asset list to be your base of operations that will keep everyone familiar with which sounds go where. Therefore, setting things up so that you can see a sound's filename pop up when the sound is played during the game, for example, is extremely helpful during the debugging and real-time mixing and mastering.

Defining your assets comes from establishing functionality, but it also comes from proactively finding out what the game will comprise. In preproduction this develops gradually, but as was demonstrated in the "Technology" section, we've already established the need for a system that not only plays footsteps but also can begin listing the possible footsteps that will be needed. The key concept to remember is this: Don't wait until people come asking for sounds to generate them. By then it's too late. Be a member of the team, not a stand-alone production house. This is true whether you're working in-house or remotely. The more you keep yourself informed about what's going on, the sooner you'll be ready to move forward at a moment's notice.

This doesn't mean you should feel the crack of the bullwhip right away. Take it slowly, and think through possible sounds carefully. Also, the moment you see a document such as a level list or an art list, read it. The valuable information it contains will guide the creation of your asset list.

Within the audio team, you'll also need to ready your guns for battle. This brings us to our final segment of preproduction.

Asset Preparation

When preparing assets, you'll need to organize them properly. Sounds, music, and voice files left lying around in a haphazard fashion can pile up into thousands of unresolved issues unless they're put in the right place. The right place is a directory structure.

Defining the directory structure

Your *directory structure* is where the assets live. It's their warm, safe, and happy home—but only if you build it that way.

This is where the asset list, that Master Control Program of game sounds, will save you a lot of time. As you categorize sections of your asset list, you should define your directory structure the same way. If your worksheet page in the asset list says *Player SFX* as it does in the previous figure, you might see a folder named *SFX*, inside of which is a folder named *Player*. See **Figure 1.7** for an example of this.

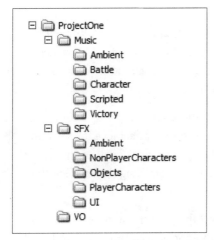

FIGURE 1.7 Creating a hier-
archical directory structure
with clearly defined categories will save you time later.

As you define your asset list, your directory structure will follow suit. This is an
easy way to keep your data organized and easy for others to follow.

Establishing a sound library

The sound library is your collection of raw material. It consists of whatever
sounds and music you compile from commercial libraries (such as Sound Ideas
or Hollywood Edge) and, more importantly, contains your own custom sounds
and music. The data is compiled by ripping your CDs and DATs to WAV data at
44.1/96 kHz and 16/32 bits or more, and keeping them in a centralized server.
Thus the sound library is your palette, not your final sound effects list. Keep in
mind that completely original sounds are part of what made *Star Wars* great.

These days, most studios use online databases that let you access sound effects
through a search engine. Some companies, such as mSoft (www.msoftinc.com),
do all the work for you, but you certainly pay for it. An alternative is to find
someone who knows FileMaker. The sound library database for Hollywood Edge
and Sound Ideas is in FileMaker format, so you can simply put the sounds into
something that's searchable online (through an intranet or the Internet) and link
it to the right files. There's also a program that can rip your CDs into data for
you, but for big libraries you need to spend a few days, if not a week or more,
swapping out CDs.

Field and Foley recording

A good chunk of your sound library will consist of canned sounds, but as I mentioned earlier, custom sounds are what will really create a fresh new feel for your title. This is achieved largely by combining and manipulating sounds from libraries, and part of this is field and Foley work.

Field recording is done by going outside your studio and capturing sounds such as ambiences. In Foley work, you record certain sounds to achieve the illusion of something else. For example, twisting and ripping apart a head of cabbage in your hands can sound like human flesh being torn. Smacking steel wire with a hammer can generate a kick-ass blaster.

Field and Foley recording should be done with the proper equipment, such as a portable DAT or digital recorder. (Digital audiotape is becoming slow and inefficient to use compared with a portable hard drive, which isn't affected by shaking or jarring and can record instantly.) You'll also need a good stereo microphone, a windscreen or two, and a large foam microphone cover. If you really want to go nuts, get yourself a parabolic dish to record far-off sounds more easily. Be sure to bring something to jot down your locations and the sounds you record. Slating (announcing) sounds helps too; otherwise you end up listening to your whole tape trying to decipher what was what. For more information on creating Foley sound effects, take a look at *Practical Art of Motion Picture Sound, Second Edition* (Focal Press, 2003).

At last, we're past preproduction! We're ready to begin hammering away at production and the nitty-gritty of the game itself.

Production

Production has fewer details to worry about than preproduction does, but that doesn't make it any easier. In the production phase, your nose is to the grindstone as you generate and implement content.

Let's take another look at the DPM. We first observe that the three categories of sound—SFX, music, and voice-over—have different elements in their workflows (integration being the most common), and the workflow of voice-over looks very similar to that of a motion picture. Keep in mind that for each category of sound, we will cover the actual creation of the sound files before we move on to integration. This doesn't follow the DPM exactly; you'll see why when we reach integration. We begin with SFX.

SFX Production

First let's take a hypothetical example of creating a sound effect. The asset spreadsheet sits before you, boggling your mind with the thousands of sound effects that still need to be created for your game. You decide that because you just saw a video file of a lightning bolt spell being cast, it'll be a good idea to tackle that sound effect next.

One lightning bolt sounds the same as another, right? Well, maybe to a buffoon. You know better. Unique sounds can create emotion just as unique music can. You immediately go into your sound effects database, which has already been set up in an easy-to-use interface for you to find and grab files. You do a search for *lightning* and pile all the results into a raw materials directory. Thus you've started to create your palette. You decide to draw from other sources—say, sweetener sounds such as heavy wood and stone impacts.

Once you have your palette, it's time to work on a canvas. For some developers, this means turning to Sound Forge (the version from either Sony or Sonic Foundry), although managing dozens of files with this program can prove time-consuming. For others, it means using Steinberg's Wavelab; for still others, Bias Peak. Each of these editors has its own set of hallmarks.

An easier method is to employ a multitracker such as Digidesign Pro Tools or Steinberg's Cubase SX (see **Figure 1.8**) or Nuendo (see **Figure 1.9**). That way you can see all the elements of each sound (an *element* being an individual sound file in the multitrack project) in addition to the effects you can put on each element all at once. Too much sweetener? Just take it down a few decibels instead of pressing Control-Z a lot and remixing in Sound Forge or Wavelab. Too much high end on one of the elements? Equalize it individually. Nothing could be simpler or more organized. If your boss is standing behind you saying, "Make it more badass," you can in mere seconds say, "Oh yeah? How's *this*?" I know you've wanted to do that for a while. Check out **Figure 1.8** to see Cubase SX's glory: You can perform multitrack editing, create sonic landscapes using MIDI, and control a great many parameters nondestructively.

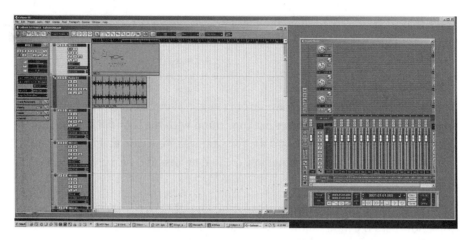

FIGURE 1.8 Cubase SX allows you to perform multitrack editing; here we see a MIDI track and an audio track being used simultaneously.

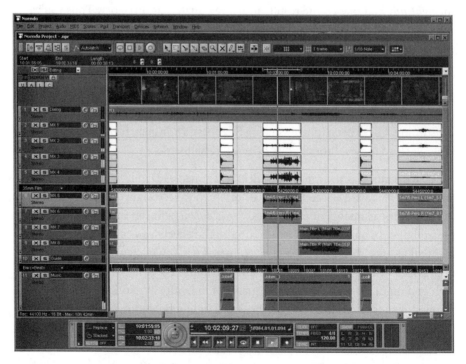

FIGURE 1.9 Multitrack editing in Nuendo is an easier and more organized undertaking than tackling file management in Sound Forge and other applications.

Note that the techniques we use in Cubase, Pro Tools, and Sound Forge are working their way into game editing environments as well. Audio engines such as Renderware Studio by Criterion give the audio team the ability to mix sound elements in real time using volume and filtering, which is much more effective. Imagine just creating all your sounds with the same parameters and adjusting them to perfection within the game itself rather than going back and forth to your multitracker. The reality of this isn't too far off. This "interactive mixing" is something we'll discuss later in more detail.

Music Production

Music production has always enjoyed a bit more popularity than sound effects production has. While sound engineers might have a sound server and a lot of recording equipment, the racks of modules and effects processors that line the walls are usually reserved for composers. Funny, these vast rooms of gear for musicians are equally important to the success of a game as the humble sound effects server is, and they all need to work together fluidly to achieve anything that sounds halfway polished.

Let's look at an example of writing a piece of music. We will explore people's aesthetic opinions of music later. For now let's just say you already know what kind of music you want to write. In the design document, the RPG calls for something "fantasy-like" and "ominous." You've thought it through and have decided that you don't want to create something completely out of the ordinary, but you don't want anything too common either. Easier said than done—but you have your *Conan, Legend, Lord of the Rings*, and *Krull* soundtracks in front of you, and you've heard what's been written before. The next step is defining your instrumentation.

Depending on your weapon of choice, you'll be using either a guitar with some sort of MIDI interface (such as an Axon) or a keyboard. Some developers even choose to bypass these and go straight for the PC interface directly, through the notation/drum map/piano roll editors of their multitrack software, through a software synthesizer, or through a "tracker," which uses samples to create MOD files (step-time composition programs, popularized by the now-15-year old Amiga PC, that competed and won over the IBM PC–based General MIDI music technology for games). Instruments can be derived from a live recording, from factory presets on your keyboard synthesizer or module, or from a software synthesizer or sampler.

What's important to remember is that you need to spend some time exploring these tools. In the '80s, the synthesizer and sampler were completely new, and bands could get away with using factory presets all the time. Now, it isn't so easy. As these tools have become more and more powerful, musicians have been encouraged to make sounds of their own. Understandably, this isn't something that everybody wants to spend their time doing. When you want to write music, sometimes you just want to write the damn music. Whip out that guitar or harmonica and start noodling away. More power to you. John Williams made his career with mostly just one instrument set. However, we all know that the orchestra can be abused only so many times by pretenders to the throne, and we need to look for new ways to sing. I recommend you budget at least a week's worth of time for searching your instrument banks and tweaking knobs and faders. You will be amazed at what you can do these days.

Now you've created your instruments. We'll explore the most ideal way to actually write the music later (see "The Fat Pipeline" in Chapter 7), but now it's time to plunge into our multitrack software and write about a minute and a half of ominous-sounding music, with low tones and a slow, dragging tempo. Why a minute and a half? Why ominous? Why a slow tempo? We'll get to that in the implementation section.

Voice-over Casting and Recording

Voice-over is a different kettle of fish entirely—a big enough kettle to warrant factoring another level of detail into our production DPM for casting alone (see **Figure 1.10**).

You can sit down and begin creating sound effects regardless of whether you have a list of the exact effects you want. The same goes for music: If you have even an inkling of a notion as to what the game type is, you can begin writing. But it doesn't hold true for dialogue. You can't say just anything and expect it to be relevant to the game. You need a script. You also need a character list.

Once the first draft of your script is complete and you have a character list, you create audition scripts. These scripts begin with a description of a character. Age and ethnicity are important to these descriptions, but so are personality traits. Avoid saying stuff like "a rogue cop with nothing to lose." Instead, be more specific; "irritable and quick-tempered" is far more helpful to an actor. The audition script should contain a few lines to read, and it's best to include short lines as well as long lines. For example, in a cut scene a character might give a speech about his belabored childhood, while in the game itself he says one-liners as well as reacts to the player in various ways. You want your actors to be able to think on their feet as well as spout out a beautiful allegory.

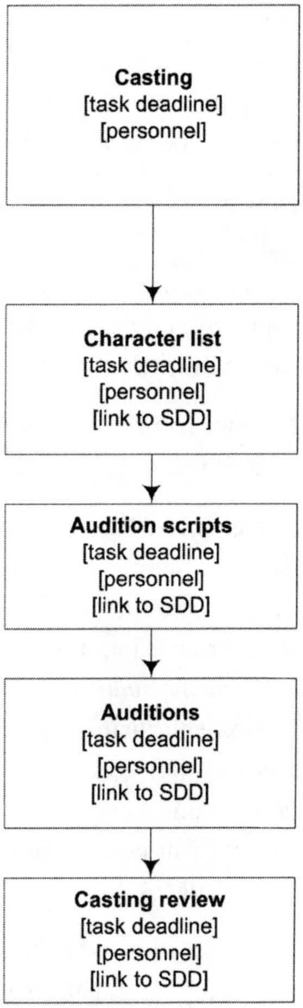

You also must decide whether to hire a casting director. This will depend on how many characters are in the game, how many lines there are, what your budget is, and what your schedule is like. Because recording sessions often don't happen until at least halfway through the project cycle, you're not likely to have spare sound designers or composers twiddling their thumbs. The audio director may be able to spare time for this task, but not if he or she is already busy providing other assets for the game. A casting director has the resources and the experience to simplify the casting process significantly. The downside is that a casting director isn't as intimate with the project as the audio director is, so you'll need to communicate your needs clearly and carefully.

No matter whether you or a casting director is in charge, let the auditions begin, and start gathering files on potential cast members. After that, the audio director, the producer, the project director, and anyone else who considers himself important will listen to the files and forward his opinion to the casting director, who will cast the characters.

Casting
[task deadline]
[personnel]

Character list
[task deadline]
[personnel]
[link to SDD]

Audition scripts
[task deadline]
[personnel]
[link to SDD]

Auditions
[task deadline]
[personnel]
[link to SDD]

Casting review
[task deadline]
[personnel]
[link to SDD]

FIGURE 1.10 The voice-over casting process is important enough to require its own level of detail within your DPM.

Fortunately, recording is a bit less complicated than casting, but you still need to prepare. Make sure you test your gear thoroughly before the first actor comes into the studio. Also make sure you back up your recordings and keep them somewhere other than your IT department. You want to be extra sure nothing gets deleted. In-house staff members who produce audio can redo things, but you don't want to have to bring actors in a second time to rerecord lines that were lost because you didn't back up your files.

Now it's time to decide on a voice director. Voice direction is a very specialized skill, so to offload it to someone in the sound department usually isn't a good idea. Find a professional, and get professional results. For these sessions it's also super helpful to have the writers in the studio to clarify the context of the lines, thus minimizing rewrites and redos.

Now we come to the technology that you'll use to actually do the recordings. For a bit of fun, here's an example of recording a line of voice-over:

The engineer (the person running the board during the session, usually a sound designer or an intern) checks the levels and makes sure the actor is reading well on the preamp. He then looks at the screen of his Mac running Mtools VoicePro. VoicePro is a handy piece of software that records individual files. Whoever is *running the board* (handling the mixing board and controlling the recording equipment during a session) presses a button; the line is sent to a screen in the studio; a red light goes on; the actor reads the line; a button is pressed again, and you're done. Saves a lot of work on editing. The engineer gives you the thumbs-up, and you nod to the actor in the studio. The button is pressed again, and the red light goes on.

The actor's line—"Help me!"—comes out like a squealing pig. Having done this many times before and knowing the context of the line, the voice director instantly says, "OK, let's do that again, only this time I want you to take it down a notch. The character, Silenus, isn't dying from a sword in his throat, he's struggling against a particularly nasty brand of poison. Make it sound more choked and gurgled, like this...." The button is pressed again, and the line comes out perfectly.

Now we've created a sound effect, we've written a piece of music, and we've recorded a line of dialogue. The easy part is done. Now it's time to implement those sounds.

Integrating SFX

As you can see in the production DPM, there are many categories of sound effects, from NPC (non-player characters) to UI/HUD (heads-up display). Well, enough of the acronyms. We'll be taking a look at the sound effect we just created, the lightning bolt spell.

Let's categorize it. According to our ever-present design document, it appears to be a spell cast by a player with a lightning bolt spell. Thus, it would go into the "Integrate player SFX" category. Let's make this sucker a level of detail (see **Figure 1.11**).

As you can see, our sound is not just a sound file anymore. A better way to handle sounds these days is by putting them into data structures. Funny for me to be talking about this, since I got a D in advanced placement computer science in high school, but that was before I knew or cared about this sort of thing. (*Cough.*) Moving on, let's briefly discuss data structures.

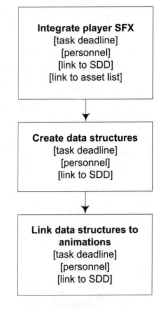

FIGURE 1.11 Additional levels of detail allow you to further define and categorize tasks.

Examples of audio data structures

Say you have a lightning bolt sound effect. You decide to implement it the old-fashioned way: giving the file to a programmer and waiting until it magically appears in the next build of the game. This can work, except that when you play the build, you notice yourself using the lightning bolt spell quite a bit. The sound plays exactly the same way again and again, over and over. Annoyed, you think, *Hmm, maybe I should send the programmer a variation of this lightning bolt sound.* Now you're using your noodle, except the problem isn't solved no matter how many sounds you give the programmer. You're not in control.

You now take the "new-fashioned" approach, where the sound designers do the integration themselves and define what they want a sound to do *before* they implement it. How about that?

So let's take a look at a lightning bolt that has four different sound files that play randomly, varying a bit in pitch and volume each time. We group these files along with this randomization behavior into a data structure. This structure is also known as a schema, a sound bank, a program, a sample—the list goes on. I personally prefer *schema* because it isn't misleading; it is a container and a template for sound files, and the *scheme* part implies that there is some plan for how those sounds work.

What's even cooler is that the sound designers can do all of this themselves! Imagine a graphical user interface (GUI, the most prevalent example of which is Windows) with a window that stores these schemas in a directory structure, a window where sound files can be loaded into a schema, and another window with randomization functionality as well as other behaviors. The sound designer creates a new schema, loads their sound files—WAV, OGG (a nifty new compression alternative to MP3), and what have you—and sets their volume, behaviors, and so forth, and the data structure process is complete. If sound designers want additional functionality, they can expand the data structure behavior (the only part of this process that requires programmer involvement), and with batch processing in place can apply behaviors to entire groups of schemas rather than hand-tweaking each one.

Such GUIs exist in proprietary engines as well as in engines such as Renderware Studio. If you think that's cool, you ain't seen nothin' yet.

Look at our production DPM again in the "Integrate play SFX" category and you'll see "Link [data] structure to animation" listed in **Figure 1.11**. This is where the übercoolness begins. Rather than even talk to a programmer, the sound designer can load up a browser that has all the characters (displayed as "meshes") in it. The designer then selects the player that has the lightning bolt spell capability. Into that same browser pops up a list of animations. The designer scrolls to the correct animation (let's assume it's "CastLightningBolt"), uses a slider to find the point in the animation at which he wants the sound to be triggered, and presses a button that says Attach Schema. He selects the schema from his own GUI, and voilà, the sound is in the game.

Now that we've done that for a sound effect, let's do it for music.

Integrating Music

Since the music you just created is environmental in nature, and therefore exists to enhance an area that the player is in rather than the actions the player performs, we can apply what we've learned about data structures to the "Integrate environment music" category of music implementation (see **Figure 1.12**).

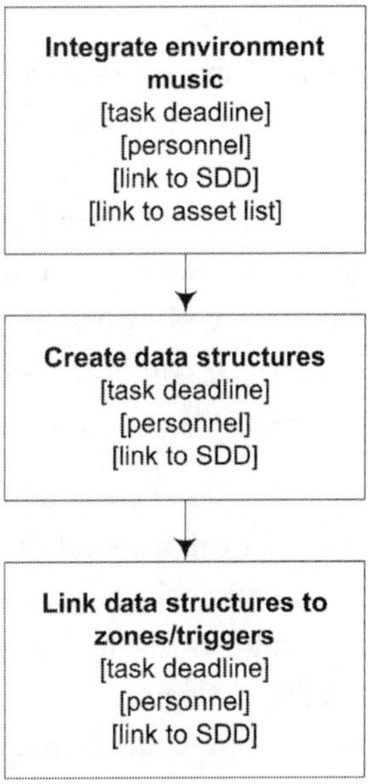

To add music to our data structure (or schema) list, we follow the same steps we would with a sound file. Pop in the music file (or files, if you want varied music to play, just as you'd want various sounds to play for your lightning bolt) and add it to the directory structure.

Because this piece of music is environmental, either the programmer must trigger it to play throughout the entire map (or level), or we must take it upon ourselves to make it the main theme of a level that can be changed at any time based on the player's

```
┌─────────────────────────┐
│  Integrate environment  │
│          music          │
│     [task deadline]     │
│       [personnel]       │
│      [link to SDD]      │
│   [link to asset list]  │
└─────────────────────────┘
            │
            ▼
┌─────────────────────────┐
│  Create data structures │
│     [task deadline]     │
│       [personnel]       │
│      [link to SDD]      │
└─────────────────────────┘
            │
            ▼
┌─────────────────────────┐
│ Link data structures to │
│      zones/triggers     │
│     [task deadline]     │
│       [personnel]       │
│      [link to SDD]      │
└─────────────────────────┘
```

FIGURE 1.12 The same process that integrates a sound effect into a data structure can also integrate music.

location. (A level is a segment of gameplay most of us are familiar with, usually consisting of a contiguous setting. Super Mario Bros., for example, used "Level 1-1" to define its levels.) The audio team, with the help of a programmer, can do this if there is a *zone system* or *trigger system* in place.

With a zone system, we delve into the same editing environment a level designer uses: the map editor. Just about any game engine, whether it's proprietary or commercial, has a map editor. The Unreal Engine has UnrealEd, and Renderware has Renderware Studio. Why do this yourself? Once the programmer provides you with a system that lets you place things into a map or level yourself, you have control of what happens from start to finish, from when the audio is created to when it goes into the game.

In your map editor, familiarize yourself with how to load a map, what various other data structures look like (a light, for example, will probably look like a candle or lightbulb icon hovering in the map or attached to an object like a street lamp), and how to navigate and orient yourself in the map.

Zone system

Before I dive into zones, you need to understand maps. A map is defined as a particular portion of the game. Since a game's graphics can't be processed all at once, it is split into chunks. The particular chunk of the environment that the player's character is in is called a map. For anyone who has played a video-game, an example of a map is a single level in Pac Man; for modern games and our work with zones, a map is a single level in a game like Doom. The sound designer or composer—whoever is integrating assets into the game—needs to place sounds and music within these maps.

In a *zone system*, you let zones identify various areas of a map that you wish to control from a sound or music perspective by creating a simplified version of a level. Rather than deal with complex shapes (which define modern maps), the integrator is free to deal with simple shapes. Let's say you have a map that uses 300,000 polygons—the geometric objects used to generate shapes in a game engine (for example, a cube is made up of six polygons). You want to define where sound goes and how it behaves so that it is reproduced as realistically as possible, but processing how sound travels and interacts with each of the 300,000 polygons would put an enormous strain on the game engine.

So to avoid overworking your processor, you create a zone system. The zones use only about 20 percent or less of the polygons but still create the same basic shapes as the map itself does. Since a zone is invisible and far less complex in shape, using it as opposed to the map geometry it represents yields nearly identical results using a fraction of the processing power. For example, for sound purposes, a cube with six sides provides the same kind of sound area that a cavern with stalactites and stalagmites shaped roughly like a cube would, whereas the cavern itself would use far more sides. This cube is our "zone."

Each of the map zones still needs to be defined, though, and in between each simplified shape is a portal or gateway, which helps define such properties as nonplayer-character pathfinding (how the nonplayer characters move in a map), lighting (how light travels), and so on. Thus, once the gateways are placed, you have a way to select each zone and give each one properties. Selecting a piece of music or a sound effect to play in the zone can be such a property. The property can be accessed by clicking on a zone and having it displayed in a window somewhere in the editing environment.

This way, whoever is editing the map for sound can select a zone and place a music-data structure in it. The music might vary by volume each time it loops; it might play multiple files; it might layer a new piece on top of an existing one—but whatever the behavior, you can control where the piece of music plays without having to go to a programmer.

Trigger system

Triggers function the same way zones do by giving whoever is editing direct control over where in the game environment a piece will play (such as a level) and where it will stop. Using this methodology, you don't need zones; you can simply place a trigger anywhere in a map, and when something collides with the trigger, the piece starts playing and will continue until the player either collides with another trigger or returns to the same one. You can also set trigger properties to continue playing a piece that was already playing in a previous location. Layering can be done with triggers as well as zones. This system is very flexible and has been used by great sound designers including Eric Brosius, who applied triggers in games like *Thief* to great advantage.

Integrating Voice

Implementing voice files is a bit easier than implementing music and sound files, but in terms of developing a reliable system it's no less complex.

You need to link the file you recorded with a character animation. But if you had to link all voice files—10,000 being the average number in a role-playing game—in the same way you link files for combat or other behaviors, you'd spend months on end doing it.

A better way is to develop a system that creates an ID for your voice file and stores it in the filename. Your recording software can name it automatically, or you can do it by hand. Once the file is in a directory structure on your local workstation, you can run a batch script (a kind programmer can easily provide this with PerlScript) that puts it in the proper place in the game build. The file will be programmed to trigger at the appropriate animation, when the corresponding text is displayed. Usually the voice-data structure contains the text from the line spoken, text that is linked to a master-conversation or voice-over editor the writers use. When a line changes, a flag is set in the software that links the voice-over editor to the voice-data structure, which notifies the writers and sound designers (either via e-mail or simply by turning the text red) that the line and the voice file are not identical.

Result

What I've just described is an example of an entire game development process for audio in today's world with a few advanced techniques. While there are quite a few other techniques not yet in general use that I'll describe later, this is still a very good way to create audio for your game. Why?

We've seen that technology isn't just about using 44.1-kHz files or licensing a hit band. Technology that makes implementation go faster can yield far higher profits because it lets you finish faster and under budget.

We've discussed the fact that multitracking your sounds gives you an edge over two-channel editors. We've also discussed that doing new things with your music and sound can yield very positive results. Everyone agrees repetition is bad, but it's still a point worth stressing. What everyone doesn't necessarily agree on is how to avoid that repetition. We'll be exploring that later, so read on.

Project management, organizational development, industrial engineering, business process reengineering—all of these are methodologies for improving how a team of people works together to create a product or a service for a profit.

Using our development process map (DPM), we've been able to outline our process visually, and we've seen that it makes life easier than a thousand-page workbook does. It's also clear that getting things right in preproduction makes life in production far more enjoyable, but only recently have audio teams been milking preproduction for even a fraction of what it's worth. In the next chapter, we'll take a look at the nitty-gritty of workflow and analyze paradigms that nonaudio staff commonly use.

CHAPTER 2
Workflow

THERE'S A LOT MORE to a plan than the plan alone. In Chapter 1, I covered the simple part: the development process map (DPM). Now I'll delve into aspects of development that are harder to document, starting with the work itself and what makes us able to do that work. Much more is involved in getting the job done than mapping it out, and we'll explore a few parts of the production cycle that most developers take for granted in a production cycle. You may expect me to start by giving you examples of a sound engine design, but that won't help you communicate a concept of your own to the programming staff, or help you know how to be in the proper mind-set before making assumptions as to what will go into the sound engine. So I begin with workflow.

Strictly defined, workflow is how actions are combined over a period of time to achieve a desired result. Obviously work doesn't happen automatically. What isn't so obvious is how to control work to make it effective. When faced with work, any member of a game production team is confronted by the need to be creative, an urge that conflicts with the need to be organized and responsible. The two seemingly opposing forces of audio and art cause the most friction. In this chapter I'll try to break down the wall between creativity and organization, so that work in an office of a ruthless giant like Electronic Arts can feel like work in the basement of a demo group house in Finland.

What's the key to bridging the gap between these two forces? *Communication.* Let's begin by taking a look at some misconceptions surrounding what an audio team consists of. In Chapter 6, "Ideal Workflow," we will right these misunderstandings by presenting team members' proper titles and describing their proper roles.

Audio Team Misconceptions

Composer/sound designer: This is the most commonly mislabeled audio staff title. Too many companies have an in-house staff member who performs the functions of a composer as well as those of a sound designer. In some cases this works well. Sound and music are scheduled separately and completed separately by one person competent enough to do both tasks or at least contribute to their completion. In most cases, however, this person is expected to do essentially everything except voice. Music and sound are becoming tasks too large for one person to take on alone; in the next few years this combined position will become obsolete.

Audio lead/director/manager: These three terms are not fully defined at every game company. Therefore, their role is not obvious. It's important to separate management tasks like scheduling and budgeting (assigned to a director or manager) from tasks that have to do with creative direction such as making sure a piece of music or sound fits with the game as a whole (assigned to a lead).

Music director: This term is used loosely. Often it applies to someone who creates music as well as licenses music written by other people (usually unsigned or independent-label bands) to include in a game. A music director should oversee all music production for a game to ensure that the soundtrack is cohesive, but he doesn't actually create any of the music unless he is uniquely qualified to do so. Music direction is a task unto itself.

Sound designer/sound engineer: A sound designer is someone who creates sounds, even though if we use the term literally it means the person designs them rather than actually creates them. A sound engineer takes created sounds and makes them work together properly.

The terms *sound* and *audio* are used interchangeably. This is acceptable.

Now that you understand how titles of audio team members can be misused, I move on to what assumptions to avoid from the perspective of various audio team members.

Challenging Assumptions

The first problem that tends to plague audio is the same problem that plagues every other part of the game: erroneous assumptions. In fact, inaccurate assumptions plague everything from what constitutes good food to what makes a good car. Assumptions are very sneaky and can easily catch a composer or even a sound designer when he or she least expects it.

We will look at some examples of inaccurate assumptions from the perspective of the audio content creator and the producer or project lead.

Producer or Project Lead Assumptions

Assumption No. 1: "A band will provide good marketing exposure for the game. The music will work great too."

This is a hot topic. Bands, both unsigned and chart-topping, are creeping into game soundtracks. The bands that love videogames are ecstatic as their record publishers flounder in the wake of widespread MP3 distribution, and games are a great way to distribute music that can't easily be ripped. Old-school composers are in an uproar.

Regardless of exposure or publicity, the most important question isn't, How much money will this make? Rather it's, Will this fit well in the game? Consider the most successful film soundtrack of all time: *Titanic*. It had a runaway No. 1 hit, "My Heart Will Go On," written by James Horner and performed by Celine Dion. What's most important about this success story is that the music worked well in the film. The film wasn't so much a historical drama as it was a romance geared toward teens and young adults, and the song fit that direction like a glove.

The game *Tiger Woods 2004* is a golf title that offers tracks ranging from DMX's "Party Up" to Rooney's "Blueside," the first being rap, the second being alternative pop. If those made the game sell better, that's great—it's hard as hell to make music a selling point for a game. However, this golf title won't go down in history as a rival to *Links* for a very good reason: None of the songs fits the gameplay. This isn't to say that a classical string quartet needs to follow golf gameplay these days, since golf is no longer exclusively a rich gentleman's game. But the radical direction taken in this particular case just didn't work. A soundtrack needs to be woven into the game smoothly.

Assumption No. 2: "A really high-profile movie composer will work well in this game."

Allow me a brief account. I was recently talking shop with a colleague of mine, Todor Fay. He created a music system that Microsoft bought and eventually turned into something called DirectMusic. While this program, released in the mid-1990s, wasn't very popular or easy to learn, it was the most revolutionary interactive music system of its day.

We were strolling in San Jose on our way to dinner when I mentioned to Todor my love of the soundtrack to *Aeon Flux*, a cult animated series first shown on MTV's *Liquid Television*. The soundtrack employed unusual compositional methods and instrumentation to generate fairly standard harmonic progressions. Simply put, the soundtrack was very new and very cool. At this, Todor turned to me and said, "I know the guy who did the soundtrack for that: Drew Neumann. We went to the same college." My heart skipped a beat. I went on to mention that a development team had been given the license to create a game based on *Aeon Flux*, using a game engine I was intimately familiar with: the Unreal engine.

Todor's eyes gleamed and his voice got more excited. "Wait a minute, you know DirectMusic and Unreal, and I know Drew! Let's have him write the soundtrack and you integrate it using DirectMusic into the game! It'll be awesome!" I was ready to burst with excitement at this prospect. As it turned out, the developer liked the idea but was obligated to use in-house staff for the work. And in the end, the game was never released.

The point of this story is that Todor's idea, like DirectMusic, was revolutionary, but only in the fact that it was taking an established score and making it adaptive. For years, hundreds of producers and project leads had visions of John Williams walking up to them and saying, "Here's the theme to your game—it'll be even better than *Star Wars!*" Even now, Danny Elfman (the composer for the movie *Batman*, among others) is working on his first game soundtrack. Again, however, it is only half of the picture: The score is just production of the music itself.

Integration of the score, especially in an adventure or role-playing game, can make the difference between a triumph and a colossal flop. Thus, thinking that a famous movie composer will make a game succeed isn't so much a bad or wrong assumption as it is an incomplete way of approaching a game's soundtrack. Think of the difference between hearing a theme unrelated to your actions in a game, and a theme that plays just to augment a dramatic moment that you generate. For example, in the game *No One Lives Forever,* when the player (as a secret agent) bungles an assassination attempt, the music plays a more dissonant segment, which connotes the disastrous result. If the player succeeds, the music becomes triumphant. Rather than experiencing the same music each time you play, you get a personalized movie soundtrack. That is what sets games apart.

Assumption No. 3: "We can program our audio engine in three months, easy."
This is a classic example of an assumption made by folks beyond just the project lead or producer. I actually was once told that it would take one programmer only about three months to complete the coding process for an audio engine of a cross-platform, cross-genre title. There would be 60 to 80 pieces of music, more than 1000 sound effects, and more than 30,000 lines of dialogue. The viewpoint was first-person (which often makes creating adaptive scores more difficult because of the conflict between standard music and the immersive element of gameplay), and the game had 100 items and more than 30 levels, with a minimum of 15 hours of gameplay.

Needless to say, the engine took far longer than three months to program. While the engine ended up being very powerful, the audio team was plagued by bugs as well as uncertainty over what features would be used and how they would integrate with other parts of the overall game engine. Add to that the fact that the programmer assigned to work on sound was needed for higher-priority coding jobs, and the result is a disorganized scheme for creating audio code. Such confusion is best avoided by designing, prototyping, testing, and locking down a workflow for audio integration, which is what this chapter is all about.

Assumption No. 4: "We need one person in charge of vocal sessions."
This statement, taken literally, is not a bad idea. Unfortunately, at times a game producer or another executive feels the need to be responsible for voice direction in a game because he or she has strong feelings about it. This is understandable, because the producer or executive is connected to the game's plot and design more intimately than the audio staff is. Nonetheless, this is a good example of an area that a manager could delegate.

Voice direction for a large-scale project would tear a producer away from other tasks for months at a time. In such cases, a separate voice director must be used, whether a member of the audio staff or a contracted professional. In general it's a good idea to use someone with experience in voice direction, although you run the risk of employing someone who doesn't know the project back to front. The producer then needs to make sure the contracted help understands and represents the project's needs adequately and doesn't follow some other agenda.

On a project with only a few lines of dialogue, a qualified producer or project lead might do some fantastic voice direction in a few sessions, and then go on their merry way to handle other project areas.

Regardless of who does the voice direction, it's crucial to have someone in charge, as well as to have the following people in the control room: the writer, the director, and the engineer. The writer can bring context to lines. The director can help lend those lines substance and proper delivery. The engineer's job is obvious: to run the board and make sure the session goes smoothly from a technical standpoint.

Here are some comments about assumptions from one of the most legendary of all project/studio leads, Warren Spector. Warren began his career in games in 1987 after having worked at TSR, a well-known maker of nonelectronic role-playing games. He has worked on some of the most groundbreaking electronic role-playing and adventure titles since then, including *Ultima 6, Ultima 7: Serpent Isle, System Shock, Ultima Underworld,* and *Deus Ex.*

Interview with Warren Spector

AB: *Would you please respond to some typical assumptions made by producers, project leads, and directors? Here's the first one: "A popular band will provide good marketing exposure for the game; the music doesn't necessarily have to be a perfect fit with the genre."*

WS: I think if you go after a name-brand act and their material is appropriate to the game you're making, you can get some mileage out of a popular band. If the band isn't big enough, you're wasting money. Regardless, in the end, I can't imagine anyone buying a game because a band has a song in it.… Even having David Bowie and Reeves Gabrels doing the entire score for *Omikron* didn't help sales and, much to my chagrin, I don't think anyone remembers Reeves' contribution to the *Deus Ex* soundtrack.…

AB: *"A high-profile film composer will work well in this game."*

WS: If you can find a composer who "gets" that games aren't movies, this can work. Or, if you get a high-profile film composer to create music that has a signature sound and then team him or her up with some audio guys who get interactive music, that can work. I mean, hearing John Williams' music in a *Star Wars* game is kind of a requirement, isn't it?

AB: *"We can program our audio engine for this RPG in three months, easy. All we need to do is match the quality of the previous title."*

WS: You always have to try to do better than that. Until the fidelity of our images and world simulations gets way better than it is now, audio is going to have to create mood and cement the illusion of reality for players. We're still in an age of games that look like cartoons—even the most realistically rendered games and most detailed characters are pale imitations of life. Audio is as central to games as it is to cartoons. Not that we always treat it that way!

AB: *"We shouldn't begin working on how audio relates to design until our design doc is finished."*

CONTINUED ▶

Interview with Warren Spector, continued

WS: That's insane. Audio should be a major component of your plan from day one. OK, that probably isn't true for all games, but for most I think it is.

AB: *What about assumptions made by audio staff? Here's one: "Everyone else is responsible for telling me what I should do. I shouldn't have to keep bothering people to ask when it's time for me to create assets."*

WS: The more tightly integrated into the team the audio department is, the better off you are. And you always want people who are invested enough to take the bull by the horns and generate stuff proactively. The audio staff *is* subject to the same creative controls everyone else on the team is—that is to say, the creative director on the project is in charge—but that doesn't mean you want people waiting to be told what to do. That applies to all disciplines, not just audio.

AB: *"Any kind of band in this game is going to suck. I should just write the music myself."*

WS: This can only be addressed on a case-by-case basis. Some games cry out for licensed music and/or band performances. Other games require unique, interactive, adaptive music that no prerecorded tracks can provide. The key for me is that music—wherever it comes from—complement the game's vibe, cement its reality for players, and not draw too much attention to itself as music. It's a mood setter and enhancer, not the main attraction.

AB: *"I can use a live orchestra now. I should do that for every game!"*

WS: Hmm. Not sure about this. As wonderful as our synths and modelers are nowadays, they're still not *quite* up to the real thing. If you can afford a live orchestra, and it's the right sound for your game—i.e., you're not doing a skateboarding game or a game about competitive roller disco—why not?

AB: *Here's the last one: "Everything sounds better when it has more bass."*

WS: Well, ask my wife and she'll agree with you! I always turn the bass way down, myself, but I think that's 'cause I've lost the high end of my hearing from cranking my '57 Les Paul Junior to 11 and standing next to a drum kit for hours on end!

Let's flip the coin and be hard on ourselves for a moment, shall we? We audio folk aren't entirely innocent.

Audio Staff Assumptions

Assumption No. 1: "Everyone is responsible for telling me what to do."

The art team needs to tell you what art is doing in the game, right? The designers should e-mail you every single time they update the design document with reference to something that might involve sound, right? Bull. This is an audio developer's first step toward apathy in the game industry, and you might as well be working as a bean counter if you want to whine about your inspiration. OK, perhaps that's a bit harsh, but it is a serious matter.

If you're a composer, consider what got you into this mess in the first place: It was your passion. You didn't need word from someone to get things done; you wrote music. You wrote and wrote and wrote, and if half of your work got canned, it didn't matter. This was a fantastic game, and your music was going to be in it. It was the opportunity you had always dreamed of.

Understandably, you want to know about the stuff you're putting sound to, but that information isn't going to find its way to you on a silver platter. If you work in-house for one of the big publishers or are contracting for them, you're getting paid well, and you're getting paid to bother people if things are to get done.

Assumption No. 2: "A band in this game is going to suck. I should just write the music myself."

For game composers who have been around the block, this is a hard concept to accept. Game music is traditionally done by a dorky white guy sitting at his computer. Well, the tradition has changed. Four years ago I collaborated with David Bowie's guitarist Reeves Gabrels on the soundtrack to *Deus Ex*. I could have gotten excited and begged to be his best friend so that I could meet Ziggy himself. I could have been rude, claiming that his music wasn't fit for games and that real game composers are the ones who should be writing, not boa-wearing pop stars. There were moments that I wanted to do both, though not at the same time, of course.

I did neither. My first glimpse into the world that makes hit records and plays to stadiums full of screaming fans was the same it would have been if I were working with a colleague with a PC and a tracker program or MIDI sequencer. Reeves was a nice guy and liked my conversions of his pieces. In fact, he said he was amazed by how much I could make a MOD file sound like his Pro Tools projects. I even made a few compositional changes that he approved of heartily.

This ties in with producer/project lead assumption No. 1, though. When a band doesn't fit in a game, that's bad. When a band *does* fit in a game, that's good. But don't assume that the game's soundtrack will sink to the depths of hell just because your lead thinks having a band is a good thing. Look at *Wipeout XL* to see what I'm talking about.

Assumption No. 3: "I can use an orchestra now! I have to use an orchestra all the time! I'm going to be the next Hans Zimmer!"

For God's sake, stop assuming this. An orchestra and all its instruments are tools. Software synthesizers such as Absynth and Reaktor are tools. You use the right tool for the job. Game soundtracks are sounding more and more like TV shows—and why? Because they *are* TV shows! Do what I did: Use an orchestra once, and move on. There's no denying the power of sitting in on a session and hearing your music played live—it's exhilarating. But do it again only if the situation really calls for it.

Assumption No. 4: "Everything sounds better punched up."

Another delusion held by all audio folk who gleefully cling to their BBE Sonic Maximizers is that all sound needs to be normalized to überhigh levels, in some cases creating a WAV file that in Sound Forge looks like a solid brick (see **Figure 2.1**). Engineers on any major commercial album or film soundtrack understand that a proper balance of dynamic and frequency range is vital to avoid butchering the ears of the average listener. If listeners want more bass, they have many ways they can tailor that to suit their own needs.

There is also the design consideration. If the player's main attack at the start of the game is too wimpy-sounding compared with an attack they might gain later in the game, there's a reason for that. There's no "going to 11" in the digital realm without distortion and clipping, so keep in mind your dynamic range and frequency range palettes while creating each and every sonic element.

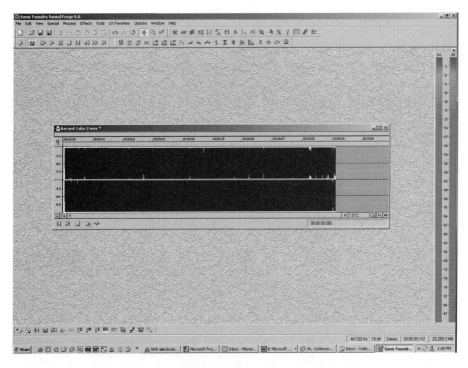

FIGURE 2.1 No self-respecting sound file should look like this, but many in fact do. A WAV file should show range, not be a solid block of data.

Also remember that sounds exist as part of a whole. Most game leads are given individual sounds to listen to before they are inserted into the game, which can be a big mistake. Separately these sounds might not seem as powerful as the leads would like, but when integrated into the game, the sounds could create a very punchy sonic environment. Giving everything more bass and more volume is not always good because it generates a bad overall mix. This is true for audio in film just as much as it is in games.

Dialogue with Audio Staff

We have seen that many paradigms about game audio are brought about by miscommunication. To get a better understanding of how this happens, let's take a look at some typical communication. The following dialogue is between the audio staff and the rest of the team, starting with the programmers.

Communicating with Programmers

Figuring out programmers' schedules

Keep in mind that a programming schedule can be incredibly dynamic. If a programmer is assigned to sound at the start of a project, it doesn't mean that he or she will be a sound programmer for the duration. If you're lucky enough to have someone assigned to sound for an entire project, that's wonderful, but in most cases it doesn't work that way, so be ready for chats like this with the lead programmer:

> *Audio Jim: Hi, Larry. I was talking to Phil, the sound programmer, and he mentioned that he's working on particle systems.*

> *Programming Lead Larry: Yeah, Jim. We discovered that upper management wasn't impressed with our effects, so we took Phil off audio for the time being. Phil and Grace will be working on particle systems together for the next month or so.*

> *Audio Jim: OK, so if I want a bug fixed?*

> *Programming Lead Larry: How urgent is it?*

> *Audio Jim: We need it fixed to finish our tasks this week.*

> *Programming Lead Larry: Oh, OK … Let me see if I can't assign it to someone else.*

> *Audio Jim: Thanks.*

What just happened here? It's clear that the sound programmer was reassigned and placed on particle systems, and that someone else would be assigned to fix a high-priority audio bug, but we can deduce far more than that:

Programming Lead Larry had his information together enough to realize that particle systems needed additional resources, but not enough to inform the sound team when the decision was made to shift the audio programmer to that system.

Audio Jim didn't make the point of the reassignment clear. Instead of just saying "Thanks" at the end of the conversation, he should have politely asked to be informed the next time a reassignment was made: "Oh, thanks; just let me know next time if there's a reassignment so I can plan for it, if you would." Granted, not all leads like being talked to like this, so you may have to adjust your tone to be either more sugary or more matter-of-fact depending on the programmer's personality.

Knowing the technology and speaking the coders' language

Something that will help you tremendously as an audio developer is understanding at least some rudimentary elements of your coder colleagues' work. As for knowing what they do, the further you go into detail, the more your artistic mind will cringe—but remember that the more you know about what needs to be done, the easier the programmers' jobs will be. In some cases, programmers will be very interested in your particular field and will have opinions you might not agree with, but count it as a blessing that they don't write off your discipline.

Here's another example of communication that can improve your life and the lives of the engineers who hold the keys to good audio implementation:

> *Programmer Paul: Hey Alan, wait a minute. Your last name is Bradley, right? Wasn't that the name of the guy in Tron?*

> *Audio Alan: No idea. That'd be freaky, though. Just think if your last name was Atreides instead of Atkins.*

> *Programmer Paul: Er, anyway, you mentioned something about "mix boxes" in this console that we're working with. I can't get anything but a buzz out of this thing at the moment using our middleware. Do I need to know about mix boxes?*

> *Audio Alan: As far as I know, according to the audio part of the SDK documentation, the console uses mix boxes with its own SDK for how it handles sounds being routed to the right channels. I can get that info for you, but how it interfaces with the middleware is something I'm not sure about.*

> *Programmer Paul: Oh, OK. Yeah, that info would be great. Thanks!*

> *Audio Alan (holding up floppy disk): This code disk means freedom!*

> *Programmer Paul: Uh, yeah … (walking away, shaking head)*

As we can see, the two have a unique fixation on the film Tron, but more importantly, the audio engineer has enough knowledge about the target platform that he can actually help the programmer get the code to work without doing too much legwork. (All he did was read the audio portion of the SDK documentation enough to understand and remember it.)

Finally, understanding the concepts of memory, streaming, diagnostics, metrics, and other medium-level audio development terms is crucial to communicating successfully with programmers.

Dealing with bad attitudes

These example conversations are fairly realistic in congenial situations. But negative chats happen as well, and a well-prepared member of the audio team will know how to deal with them. Beyond the standard one- and two-liners involving four-letter words, there are better ways to respond to clear disdain from a programmer. Here's an example:

> *Audio Arthur: Hey, I was wondering if you checked out that weapon I e-mailed you about a couple of days ago.*

> *Programmer Paula: Yeah, I made it so that the gun played a sound for each shot.*

> *Audio Arthur: Right; that's because if a designer wants the rate changed, the sounds will match no matter what. Problem is, it sounds really bad. I brought an example of a loop you can use instead.*

> *Programmer Paula: I don't want to do that. It'd mean more work later. This works best.*

> *Audio Arthur: Actually it would mean very little work now and no work later, and the sound …*

> *Programmer Paula: Dude, I don't have that in my schedule. If you want me to do it, talk to Lead. This is not a high priority.*

> *Audio Arthur: OK. Fine. (Walks away, shaking head.)*

What's happening here? The programmer is clearly doing something her own way and is not interested in hearing alternatives. One way of dealing with this is by escalating the situation with heated words, but that's not usually the right way. A few programmers out there might listen if you open fire point-blank, but oftentimes that just leads to a counterattack.

A better solution is what the programmer herself suggested: to take it to Lead. The issue has to be identified as important enough to add to the schedule somewhere. If it's just before E3 (the Electronic Entertainment Expo, the largest annual game convention in the world) and your pocket machine gun will sound like 1990 if it isn't made into a loop, the issue can be more pressing than if you're at the start of your development cycle.

The best solution? Something that isn't even mentioned: to identify the behavior that will be used for the weapon before any programmer takes action on it. This avoids wasted time and wasted effort. Spec your object behaviors for sound with the designers before any code is written.

Communicating with Artists

Art and audio are seen as polar opposites, but that's a misconception. While the two don't interact as much as audio and programming do, art can be a valuable source of feedback, early information, and in some cases direct help with various audio systems—such as anything that uses textures or animations.

A lot of art is getting shifted to preproduction in what's known as a conceptual phase. During this phase, the audio team can latch onto the concept art and use it, as well as design documents to create the concept for music and sound.

An example of dialogue between an artist and an audio engineer or composer isn't as easy to come by, but the same rules apply when it comes to knowing your terminology. Here's an example of a discussion of a surface system that identifies texture materials and plays the right footstep sounds.

Audio Andrew: Say, you wouldn't happen to know why the footsteps for metal are playing on the wooden floor texture, would you?

Art Antonio: No idea, but you should check the properties of the texture. Do you know how to do that?

Audio Andrew: Nope.

Art Antonio: OK, just go into the Texture menu and right-click the appropriate texture, then look in the field that reads Sound Property. Make sure it's assigned correctly.

Audio Andrew: Awesome; how do I get to the Texture menu?

Art Antonio: You audio guys really are dumb, aren't you? Just kidding. (Laughs.) Just go to the top-right part of the screen and click the Browsers menu.

Audio Andrew: Thanks! No offense taken; at least I didn't whip out a calculator when I had to pay the $1.17 tip last week. We all have our moments.

We've learned from this conversation that there was an implementation process that the audio engineer wasn't fully aware of but the artist was. Most of the time the programmers are the ones giving the instructions on how to use these systems, but even they might not know little secrets about their own systems, and an artist might know a shortcut.

You'll also find artists very helpful when it comes to requesting various hookup tools from the programming team. For example, you would waste an inordinate amount of time if you had to stand over an artist's shoulder while he or she thumbed through the frames in an animation and wrote down each appropriate frame number to tell a programmer where a sound should be triggered. That same artist would much prefer you to see the frames of the animation yourself in the game engine (in a fashion similar to the way you browse textures) and assign sound files to animations yourself.

Communicating with Writers

On larger game titles, the writers are the gatekeepers of the dialogue. They are the ones who provide context to the lines you need to record, and communication between the writing team and audio team is essential for good delivery. Without context, a line can sound like a dubbed Japanimation flick, and God help us if too many more games end up sounding like that.

However, writers aren't voice directors. The voice director is the one who uses the context given by the writers to make the dialogue plausible and dramatic.

Depending on the nature of the game you're working on, a line can sound dreadful no matter how it's spoken. Here's an example of the writer and voice director finding a good compromise during a vocal session. It's in this session that you hear the lines spoken for the first time by the actors you hire.

Actor Ansel: "Holy cow, where did that come from?"

Director Don: OK, that was pretty awful. [*Turning to writer.*] You say that the character is ducking from a missile shot, is that correct?

Writer Wendy: Yeah, he's taken by surprise because the area is supposed to be neutral.

Director Don: OK, and the scene is 500 years in the future, right?

Writer Wendy: Yes.

Director Don: Would it be possible to change "Holy cow" to something a little more realistic? I can have the actor read this line as is, but it will sound out of place when you hear it in the game. I doubt anyone would be saying "Holy cow" 500 years from now in a postapocalyptic society.

Writer Wendy: Sure, what do you think would work?

Director Don: Depends on the character. What's his background?

Writer Wendy: Well, he's a fairly well-brought-up young man from the wealthy part of the planet, but he was expelled from school for being insubordinate during the latter part of childhood.

Director Don: Do you think a swear word would be appropriate?

Writer Wendy: It'd work for the character, but the producer will have to make that call as I'm not sure what rating we're shooting for.

Note: A game with adult content is given a rating of M, which is similar to a rating of R for a movie.

Director Don: OK, we'll try a few "my God" lines, a few "damn" lines, a few "shit" lines, and a few yells in place of words, and we'll choose between them.

Writer Wendy: Sounds good to me.

As you can see, a healthy compromise can achieve better lines and more effective delivery. Since voice acting in games is still in its infancy, I urge all audio directors, producers, and anyone else involved in this process to realize just how bad it can be when a line isn't considered carefully when it's written and later when it's recorded. Get a good voice director, a good writer, and a good actor, and do not compromise this part of the project by making do with untested in-house talent.

Now that we've seen examples of how to communicate with various members of the production team, it's time to delve into how to communicate with management.

Scheduling from Preproduction to Postproduction

I'm repeating myself here, but it's for a good reason (no, I'm not senile). One of the biggest assumptions made by all sectors of product management is that audio does not take a very active role until production begins. This isn't true. Audio can (and should) take just as active a role as the other disciplines do. For this to happen, the audio manager or director needs to schedule properly to ensure that the means of production are in place by the time that part of the schedule is reached. Scheduling, like communication, is one of the foundations of good workflow.

We've already seen a good chunk of what happens during preproduction in our development process map in Chapter 1, "A Development Process Map of Game-Audio Implementation." We've even looked at an example of a good audio meeting that takes place early in the process. All that remains is figuring out the work that goes with making sure the DPM is followed properly. For that I will write a schedule, define a good infrastructure, and then identify tasks that support the completion of the development process.

Preproduction Nitty-Gritty

How to write a schedule
Schedules are not easy to write. One might argue that it's easier to write a book than to write a schedule. However, like the DPM, a preproduction-to-production schedule can be presented visually in a format such as a flowchart or organizational chart rather than just as a list of text. In fact, the DPM can serve as its own schedule. We've already partially done this by giving each task in the DPM a deadline (shown under "task deadline" in Figure 1.10 in Chapter 1, for example), but this doesn't allow us to track progress.

In order to track tasks consistently, keeping a list of tasks really is the best way to go sometimes. You could then link this list to your DPM. This kind of task list can be created easily in such programs as Microsoft Project.

My recommendation that follows is supported by many other sources, from commercially available management-training programs to the proprietary management documents of Fortune 500 companies. The fundamentals are the same and can be followed in a step-by-step process:

1   Write down all your tasks, regardless of whether their priority is urgent, important, or low.

2   Organize your tasks according to priority.

3   Estimate the length of each task to the best of your ability, and give each task a deadline.

4   As tasks are completed, document how long they took and whether they were completed as planned.

Repeat steps 1 through 4 as often as necessary when tasks are reevaluated throughout the development cycle.

Once you've done all this, you have a basic schedule and task-tracking system set up. Microsoft Project lets you assign each task a priority and a deadline and lay it all out visually in what is known as a Gantt chart. Such a chart is rather large and is not as elegant as a Visio-based DPM document, but it can help you more easily identify how long tasks take in relation to each other.

We now have the beginnings of our schedule! What we haven't yet figured out is how these tasks will be completed. So let's take a look at our audio team's infrastructure.

Infrastructure

In order to decide how an audio department will be set up, we first need to define its infrastructure. This is a 50-cent word that I didn't fully understand until I looked it up. Here's Merriam-Webster's definition: the underlying foundation or basic framework (as of a system or organization). Yep, that sums up what we're talking about. Developing an infrastructure is an operational task (we will get to that in a minute), and for this, we should ask the following questions, all of which relate to our scheduling process:

1   How many projects are there?

2   What kinds of projects are they?

3   How long will the projects last?

4   What kind of budget is available?

5   What kind of assets will be needed?

6   Approximately how many of each asset will be needed?

The answers to all of these questions will give you a good idea of how much equipment you will need, how much staff you will need, and when the staff will be needed. These answers can serve as the building blocks of your infrastructure development.

Once you've identified the department's basic requirements, you can document them in your schedule.

Operational tasks

Once your infrastructure is formed, you can start a list of operational tasks. An operational task is something that helps the audio department implement the work laid out in the DPM. You can add these tasks to your DPM or keep them in a separate document that you link to the DPM. This category can comprise anything from hiring more sound designers to ordering more gear. Here are some examples in specific areas of preproduction:

▶   Lead time: This allows the head of audio to run the department and can be used for scheduling, budgeting, staff meetings, documentation work, and work with other departments (such as programming and design).

▶   Purchasing: This covers the software or hardware you need to buy in order to create the audio. Hardware can even include pens and paper.

▶   R&D: During preproduction, it's very important to figure out what you need to do in order to create the right "vibe" for the game. This task includes listening to reference soundtracks, performing field recording and Foley work, experimenting with sounds and instrumentation in a multitracker, using adaptive techniques, and most importantly, playing games that relate to yours.

▶ Prototyping: When thinking of ways to incorporate audio into a game, it's important to be able to demonstrate how that audio will work, even though it may not behave or sound exactly as it will in the game. Rough prototypes can be generated in multitrack programs like Cubase SX or Pro Tools, so that an audio lead can easily produce an example of his or her plans. This is a much more effective approach than using a textual description when trying to convince others on the team of the validity of an audio design.

Now that we've rounded out preproduction workflow with a support structure for the DPM, we'll do the same for production.

Production Cycle

Just as a schedule is used to plan production, a schedule is also used to track production according to the plan. Since this is a young industry, tasks often get steered from the original plan in very different directions. This is good for managers to keep in mind to allow for flexibility in readjusting or reassessing the production schedule. And as the industry matures along with its people, scheduling is starting to be taken much more seriously as a fundamental element of a successful project.

Don't misunderstand me when I say that planning and tracking are of paramount importance. If you live with your parents and have a group of friends who want to make a game over a three- or four-year period, by all means go at it without a plan and see what happens. Often a team will feel tremendous inspiration and work very hard to create an excellent first product. After that, the inspiration fades a bit with each product, and the desire to organize the development process increases. These two factors can influence a team right out of the market if the group isn't careful, so let's take a look at how to best stay on track without losing inspiration.

The churning process

When production begins, it's noses to the grindstone. This is a time when something is created or is in the process of being created each day.

How much time does it take, on average, to create a sound effect or a piece of music? This kind of thing is hard to predict and easy to mandate, but if a fully qualified sound designer takes longer than one day to create the sound of a standard-size oak door opening, there's a problem. During production, an average to shoot for is three to five sound effects for one person in an 8-hour day, allowing for revisions after the initial sound set is created. If two people are working, this comes out to around 220 sound effects per month. This is true whether the sound designers are in-house or outsourced. For a small title such as a puzzle game or even a fighting game, this is plenty. For a large title such as an RPG or an MMORPG (massively multiplayer online role-playing game), this may be a pitiful amount (the number of sound effects can go above 2000 in some cases). Having those infrastructure questions answered will go a long way to figuring out how many staff members will be needed and for how long.

Something that helps break up the routine of daily creation is playing the games, listening to the soundtracks, and watching the movies mentioned earlier. Sometimes a designer has no idea how to create a certain sound (the equivalent of writer's block), which can be incredibly frustrating. While drawing inspiration from films and other games can be misinterpreted as stealing, sometimes this is the absolute best way to get creativity in motion, as it serves as a launchpad—a research device, if you will—to give your ideas better context.

Another method to help keep the churn burning is pure and wild experimentation. For example, go into a soft synth like Absynth or Reaktor and start tweaking knobs and sliders. Go crazy trying anything and everything. When you find a sound you like, don't just move on; save it and document it for later. Sometimes incredibly good and completely original sounds can emerge from this process.

Being aware of dependencies

In Chapter 1 we defined a dependency as something that you rely on to complete your work, whether it's a tool or a colleague. It's not always easy to identify interpersonal dependencies. The most challenging issue to resolve with your colleagues is how you will integrate your sound and hear it in a game. Another head-scratcher is figuring out what sounds are needed for things in the game that aren't described adequately. Let's tackle a few of these issues by looking at various ways to deal with them.

Design Dependencies Imagine that after reading a design document, you discover you need to create sounds for a goblin and a goblin magi. If the document lists only their names, hit points, and locations (that is, you have no sound specs), the following information for each NPC (nonplayer character) type should be identified:

▶ Size of goblin

▶ Armor, if any

▶ Attack types (Will it use bows? swords?)

▶ Footsteps (Should it be stealthy or loud?)

▶ Magic spells (What will the magi do?)

▶ Additional actions (Will it speak? jump?)

You have two ways to get this information. One is to ask the lead sound designer and then, based on what you find out, create a variety of sounds (for example, a description such as "heavy armor" could mean heavy chain mail or heavy plate mail; the sound designer should have both sounds prepared in advance). Another method—the better one—is to check out the animations of the character itself in the game engine. In a method similar to the way you browse textures, you should be able to browse character animations and meshes (meshes being the characters themselves, made up of a "mesh" of polygons).

Technology Dependencies Once you've created the two goblins' sounds, after looking at the animations or discussing it with the lead designer, you need to decide how you will attach sounds to the goblins' animations.

There are again two ways to do this—a hard way and an easier way.

The hard way is to ask the lead programmer whether anyone can be responsible (or has already been give the responsibility) to assign sounds to the animations. You can then send the appropriate programmer an e-mail with the character name, the animation name, the animation frame number, and the file to be played when the frame plays. Sometimes artists also assign sounds to animations.

The easier way is to use a system in which you can browse animations and attach sounds to the proper frame yourself. Such a system can be programmed in a relatively short period of time, depending on the underlying code and the engine the programming team is using—but in a cost-benefit analysis, the amount of time a programmer spends to create such a system will be very little compared with the additional amount of time and money that would be required to do it the hard way.

Regular and proper feedback

You can't read minds, and all the industry experience in the world won't help you much when it comes to deciphering the grand dream of a design team—especially for a complex game. That is why we use feedback, which can be either useful or a complete waste of time.

First, remember that nonaudio folk are, well, nonaudio folk. Just as you might not understand what a membrane shader is, a graphic artist might not understand what a frequency range is. So take the time to explain the terms that are necessary to help someone give you good feedback. If someone talks about increasing the bass in a sound but it's already maxed out, summarize the situation without using jargon. Explain that increasing the bass would distort the sound beyond recognition; if you tell him that his mids will go down the toilet, he might think you're talking about a new kind of drug.

Second, take feedback just as you would take any other kind of criticism. Make sure that if you don't follow up on someone's feedback, you explain why. Unless you take each piece of feedback seriously, people will doubt your willingness to change.

Finally, organize your feedback. Put all your e-mails in a feedback folder and refer to it regularly so you can identify what feedback is most important.

Defining Postproduction

We haven't mentioned postproduction until now because to the rest of the team it isn't considered part of the development process. However, it does exist in the audio team's schedule, and eventually we will see it more widely becoming part of game development—for more than just audio (as is already the case at Electronic Arts). We will discuss what happens in this inner sanctum of game audio.

Active Listening

As pieces of audio are integrated during the production phase, members of the game team listen to sounds but focus only on the ones that catch their attention. Sounds can even be disregarded entirely, as the non-audio staff concentrates on other aspects of the game such as graphics or NPC behavior code. Music can be disregarded as well, as designers or quality assurance (QA) staff sometimes play-test to their own music. This practice is perfectly common. However, as the game moves closer to completion and audio is rounded out, this approach is less acceptable. What needs to start happening well before the end of production is active listening.

Active listening involves sitting down and isolating yourself from other sounds, then playing the game with paper and pen in hand. It If anything stands out positively or negatively, even to a small degree, write it down. For example, if you find a sound to be a bit too loud, write it down, even though the sound may not be bothersome. You then go over your list and consider what is realistic to present for any kind of change request. That will be determined by keeping an eye on the schedule and knowing what the team leads (including the audio lead) consider to be important at each stage of development. Once you've narrowed your list of concerns, enter it into the database in which the game's bugs are kept (see "Bug Databases," later in this chapter). All members of the team should be scheduled to spend at least a few days playing the game while listening actively.

You might say that this technique is not as good as a blind test, in which people comment only on what stands out in a standard gameplay session. But active listening is an effective technique because it acts as a more focused standard gameplay session. Sound problems that might not stand out right away do so after repetition; with active listening, they are caught more quickly and therefore fixed more quickly.

Some forward-thinking sound designers (Guy Whitmore included) hire staff as interns to play through a game during various stages of production to listen for any audio bugs or audio-related problems. Such a position, called the audio QA and/or audio mixer, is considered in the schedule from the beginning. This forward-thinking concept can lead to a tremendous increase in audio quality—more so than if the entire audio team and QA staff are charged with general-purpose audio feedback.

The Quality Assurance Link

Just about every large game company has a QA department. It is made up of
people devoted to going through the game once it has reached a stage of basic
playability. This group can be a tremendous resource for audio in the final stages
of production.

Bug databases

The most effective way to use QA—indeed the most effective way to keep track
of anybody's comments or problems about anything in the game—is through
a bug database. The bug database is a system that allows you to record a bug
(anything from an aesthetic issue to a game crash), assign it to the appropriate
person (usually a lead such as a producer), and track its progress. Examples of
commercial database systems are Bugzilla, BugCollector, and TestTrack Pro (see
Figure 2.2).

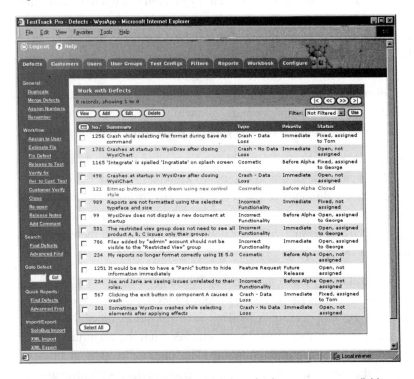

FIGURE 2.2 TestTrack Pro, one of the many bug database programs available.
Such programs are extremely important to track problems (bugs) during production.
The larger the project, the more important it is to have a well-organized database.

With a bug database, you can set up part of QA's schedule to specifically test audio issues, and at the same time plan time for members of the audio team to address bugs that QA records in the database.

The QA department can also help by collecting information about bugs that the audio team and/or programming team can't accommodate in their schedule. For example, if a bug report notes that footstep sounds aren't corresponding with a certain surface, the QA team can find out whether this happens all the time or just some of the time, and what criteria can be linked with the incorrectly triggered sounds. The QA team can also make great use of diagnostic tools, which we will explore in the next chapter—for now, just keep in mind that these tools spit out valuable information about what the game engine is doing at all times.

Matching Producer and Audio Team Satisfaction

An essential part of the latter days of production is getting the audio as close as possible to what everyone wants. This requires plenty of compromise between the audio staff and the rest of the team, and indeed between everyone involved in the project. However, the bottom line belongs to the producer or the director of development—whoever makes sure things are done on time and within budget.

The game's producer, like everyone else, has a hard job. But the producer's job is probably more difficult than everyone else's because he or she has to be familiar with everything going on, and not just superficially. The producer must understand as much detail as necessary about the way the audio team works to help solve problems as intelligently and quickly as possible. That's quite a tall order.

First, the members of the audio team can make sure their work is on the right track by communicating effectively with the producer. This is best done by a representative of the team—an audio manager or director, someone who understands audio and can clearly communicate the audio team's needs to the producer as well as translate the requirements of the project budget and timeline to the audio team. Specifically, the audio manager or director needs to communicate to the producer the audio developers' needs, from time estimates to qualitative information such as what is required to make a particular sound effective. This kind of communication ensures that the producer won't need to understand absolutely everything (such as how to use equalization tools) but will have a point of contact for explaining the essentials of what needs to be done.

Once the audio team understands the limitations of its budget and timeline, and the producer can help change the budget and timeline to ensure that the sound team is given enough of both to meet the needs of the game, work flows much more smoothly.

We've taken workflow and torn it apart in this chapter, haven't we? Rather than bore you with charts and graphs, I've tried to describe situations that really happen in order to help you deal with incorrect assumptions, miscommunications, scheduling challenges, and misunderstandings about your colleagues' responsibilities. You should now be sufficiently armed to discuss the work itself with the rest of the team and get it done more smoothly. Having said that, let's delve into the work, starting with technology.

CHAPTER 3
Technology

TECHNOLOGY is what will drive your creation, and as such it must be defined early in the development process. An important thing to consider out of the gate is what kind of sound engine will be used—middleware or a proprietary system. Let's assess each of these terms before we proceed.

A *sound engine* is all the code in a game that has to do with playing sound. It includes the low-level code that links the higher-level functions with the hardware (a PC or console). It also includes the middle-level code that drives basic playback functionality—such as what sounds are driven to what speakers, and what sounds take priority in playback based on the restrictions of the low-level code and hardware. It also includes high-level code that the sound designers use to implement the sound into the game and advanced behaviors such as adaptive soundtracks.

Middleware is a type of sound engine that a company or team buys in order to achieve extended functionality for the systems developers want to program without coding it themselves. Middleware can be a complete game engine or a portion of it that performs only certain functions (for our purposes, sound). An advantage to middleware is that a lot of work is done for you. A disadvantage is that if you want anything changed, you have to either learn a completely new code base yourself or have the middleware vendor make the change, which may take longer than if you had programmed your own system from the start.

A *proprietary system* is one that a company or team programs entirely by itself. Naturally, the advantage of this kind of system is having complete control over your code. The disadvantage is that it requires a lot more work.

Let's discuss some middleware options.

Middleware and Vendors

Middleware can make life incredibly easy for you and your sound team—as long as it does what you want it to do. Remember the development process map (DPM). Once you've established your sound engine needs, you can look at the various middleware options available and pick the one that works best for you. You also need to talk with vendors to see who you think will work with you most effectively. Here are some of the most commonly used middleware products today:

Microsoft DirectSound and DirectMusic (Go to www.microsoft.com/
windows/directx and search for DirectMusic/DirectSound)
DirectSound and DirectMusic are part of Microsoft's no-cost DirectX program,
which lets Windows-based PCs take advantage of advanced code dedicated to
multimedia applications such as games.

DirectSound is used mostly by programmers who want access to its application
programming interface (API) to play back sounds. DirectMusic has its own API
for music playback, and it also has an editing environment, called DirectMusic
Producer, for writing music.

DirectMusic deserves special recognition because it's the first freely available
software that allows users to create adaptive soundtracks. Although its interface is said to have a considerable learning curve, the system has been used to
great advantage by renowned composers such as Guy Whitmore, who did the
soundtracks for *No One Lives Forever* and *No One Lives Forever 2.*

RAD Miles Sound System www.radgametools.com/miles.htm
The Miles Sound System is an all-purpose sound system with cross-platform
compatibility. I say "all-purpose" because it uses a number of methods to play
back music and sound, but it doesn't have separate systems tailored for music
and sound the way DirectX does. This system has been around awhile; it was
created by legendary programmer John Miles in 1991. From its inception it was
supported directly by its creator and its technical support was first-rate. By all
accounts, the engine's technical support is still very strong, but its functionality
has fallen a bit behind the times. While the Miles Sound System supports fairly
current playback formats such as MP3, many compression schemes are supplant-
ing MP3 with better quality and higher compression ratios. (MP3 does best at a
compression ratio of around 7:1, but some formats can now equal that quality
at 11:1 or more.) Furthermore, as of this writing Miles does not yet support the
Nintendo GameCube or Sony PlayStation 2, according to the company's Web
site, and those systems make up a good portion of the console market. Since
many companies are going multiplatform, this is something of a hindrance.
Nonetheless, rumors of an upcoming Miles version 3 (the current version is 2),
with huge changes and improvements to its functionality, are heating up. We'll
see what RAD Game Tools has up its sleeve.

Sensaura GameCODA www.gamecoda.com

GameCODA's functionality is more advanced than Miles', but as the engine is a relative newcomer to the middleware battlefield, its support system has yet to be verified (see **Figure 3.1**). Nevertheless, its list of features is impressive. Not only does it contain the low-level code to interface with all current major platforms (Nintendo GameCube, Sony PlayStation 2, Microsoft Xbox, and the PC, as of this writing), but it also contains advanced functionality to let sounds be manipulated in all sorts of interesting ways. For example, you can manipulate sound geometry—the primitive shapes such as cubes and spheres that can represent an area in which sound plays in a three-dimensional game world—within 3D rendering programs. (This is not exactly an intuitive addition, considering that sound folks don't use 3D rendering programs as a matter of course—but it's forward-thinking nonetheless.) Also you can create sound matrices to let sounds be mixed according to various behaviors the engineer specifies, such as playback randomization and priority. To sum up, the GameCODA engine is sufficient for a simple title (such as a puzzle or fighting game) and meets almost all the needs of a complex title (such as an adventure or role-playing game).

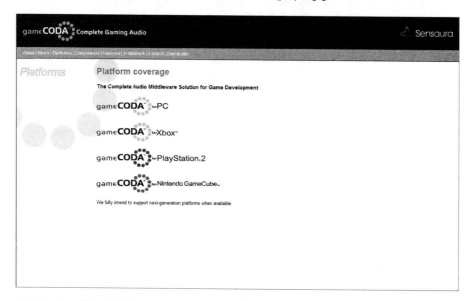

FIGURE 3.1 GameCODA is a relatively new middleware audio solution.

Creative EAX http://eax.creative.com

Creative's Environmental Audio Extensions, or EAX, is not an all-in-one sound engine. It provides advanced reverb algorithms that interface with its Sound Blaster sound card line to create decent reverb for free. As EAX has been around for quite a while (at least 1998), it has become a good-sounding system—but still not quite up to the sound that a quality Lexicon reverb can generate. EAX's advantage over Lexicon is the ability to change the reverb as a player goes from one area to another, morphing smoothly; the Lexicon reverb must remain static in a file and isn't flexible in real time. Keep in mind that Creative dominates the market for home-computer sound cards, but by no means does this cover all sound solutions for home PCs. Game developers usually employ Microsoft's DirectSound as a fallback to play sound when EAX extensions are not available to use with Creative hardware.

Analog Devices SoundMAX www.soundmax.com

SoundMAX, another specialized middleware product, was introduced as a way to synthesize sounds in real time, which was an extremely bold move. The thinking was: If visuals could be rendered in real time, why couldn't sound? This proved to generate very realistic sounds such as footsteps, water, car engines, and other specific objects whose sounds lent themselves to Analog Devices' algorithms. Sadly, the product didn't get very far, because synthesizing realistic sounds in real time still has a long way to go. I've included it here because it was one of the most advanced systems to be attempted (it's still available to whoever wants it), and other systems like it will emerge over the next five years with even more exciting possibilities. Imagine a real-sounding voice that didn't come from an actor recording lines? Such a capability isn't too far away.

All of these middleware products have strong points, but sometimes developers need to create their own engine; in the next section we'll investigate the logistics of doing so.

Custom-Made Tools

Much like any other aspect of development, custom-made tools can yield great success or incredible nightmares. Let's take a look at a custom-made engine that was originally designed for use with the game *Unreal* by Epic Games and Digital Extremes. The engine, called the Galaxy Sound System, was programmed by Carlo Vogelsang, formerly a contract programmer for Epic Games who now works at Creative.

Galaxy Development Cycle in Brief

The Galaxy Sound System was designed to take advantage of software and hardware; at the time it was developed, new products known as hardware-accelerated 3D cards—manufactured by a company called 3dfx—were starting to show up. (The market for hardware-accelerated cards is now defunct, but the technology eventually worked its way into video cards.) A consumer rift appeared between players who had such accelerator cards and those who didn't. Epic Games and Digital Extremes, *Unreal*'s codevelopers, wanted to cover as much of the market as possible, and that goal permeated all parts of the game. As a result, the game supported EAX and Aureal technology (the latter being a now-obsolete hardware-based 3D surround-sound technology).

Unfortunately, Galaxy was subject to a number of development woes. First, the development cycle for *Unreal* was roughly four years long, from 1994 to 1997, and a great deal was changing during that time. General MIDI music was on its way out, and MOD-based music as well as CD Redbook-format streamed music was on its way in. Additionally, 8-bit resolution was giving way to 16 bits. EAX was introduced, and DirectSound in conjunction with the Interactive Audio Special Interest Group introduced 3D positioning with I3DL1, its software-based sound propagation standard. This was perhaps the greatest fundamental shift in game sound technology, but it did not bode well for the sound engine.

Half of the samples of the game ended up as 8-bit audio due to restrictions on hard disk space and RAM. Because it was too late for Galaxy's programmer to take advantage of interactive streamed audio, the game ended up with a very simplified adaptive-audio MOD playback system, which triggered groups of patterns to play and loop depending on what level the designer desired. To complicate matters, the programmer was based in Holland, so the time difference and physical distance made it difficult for developers to collaborate with him on the engine's design and get response to feedback. Furthermore, there was no structure in place for the audio providers of the game to communicate sound engine issues (such as the late adoption of 16-bit sound) in a way that would prioritize them and get them either taken care of in a timely manner or dropped for higher-priority tasks.

Some simple lessons can be learned from the development of Galaxy:

▶   Make sure you schedule sufficient time to program the sound engine and prioritize tasks related to the sound engine.

▶   Make sure you know what the functionality and target hardware will be before you begin, and allow for expandability.

▶   If you have only one programmer coding a custom engine throughout the product's development cycle, provide extra support for testing and optimizing the engine.

If you keep these three guidelines in mind, you can create a sound system that is extremely robust (it won't crash easily) and at the same time flexible (it will meet different design needs and changes).

Now for comparison, I will look at the development of an ideal in-house sound engine.

Modern Sound Engine in Brief

Remember that these days, even with all the enhancements a sound engine has, it is still a lower-risk component of the overall game engine than something like an animation system, a rendering system, or a nonplayer character (NPC) system. Keep in mind that work may not begin right away on the sound engine, which is all the more reason to have a solid preproduction asset-building plan in your schedule.

High-Level Scheduling

I'll begin by taking an hypothetical development cycle that is carved in stone from the beginning. *Unreal* did not have that, but it was born out of a system that assumed delays would occur and profits would be huge as long as there wasn't too much delay.

Let's take an average development cycle time of two years and carve out six months of development time for one programmer in that period. There will be an additional three months or so of optimization (bug fixes and troubleshooting) to make sure the engine is suitable for speedy asset integration so the content producers can work quickly to implement their work. All of this is done in-house.

For a team that is not contained under one roof, such as *Unreal*'s, programming an engine can be much more time-consuming, as development cannot be coordinated as quickly as it can when everybody can meet together. E-mail is a fine invention, but it is nowhere near as effective as a meeting with visual aids. At the end of development, in fact, *Unreal* codevelopers Epic Games and Digital Extremes were running short on time and met in Canada (the location of Digital Extremes' offices) to complete the game together so that the key developers could be in one place for easier communication and problem solving. It proved an effective strategy: The game met the publisher's shipping deadline. This doesn't mean you have to rent a $5000-per-month office space in order to have an efficient team workflow, but it does mean your entire team is better off being in the same physical location for a good portion of development.

Sound engine design

Before work begins, the sound team identifies the sound engine's functionality. This process requires focusing on two areas: the needs of the current product and the needs of future products. The simplest way to consider both factors at the same time is to make an absolutely killer engine for the current product that will be suitable for future ones without showing its age. For example, rather than settle on Dolby Digital for surround, developers could program the engine to support all possible surround formats as well as any new ones on the horizon.

While designing the sound engine, the sound team must also consider the needs of the other parts of the project from a workflow perspective. Consider how you are going to integrate your sounds and music and what dependencies you have, and go from there.

First, define functionality for the benefit of the programmers as well as the audio engineers. The engine needs to be simplified in its code structure, and it must be commented on and documented properly so other programmers can figure out problems if need be. The interface also needs to be designed so that the audio folks don't run crying to the programmers whenever there's an issue. The programmers should talk to the audio team about what needs to be done as much as possible before a single line of code is written, while also keeping deadlines in mind.

Optimization

When a system is ready for testing, you should be ready to tear it apart. Testing should not involve a bunch of e-mails being sent back and forth between the programming and audio teams. Each system, from the music-playback scripting to the 3D sound propagation, should have a comprehensive list of issues stored in the bug database I mentioned in Chapter 2, "Workflow." It is the programmers' responsibility to take that list and go over it with the programming lead (responsible for all programmer scheduling and reporting to the project lead and producers) as well as the project lead and the audio team to assess what will take priority.

Diagnostics and metrics

Until recently, a bug would be reported and a programmer would have to duplicate it to see what went wrong. That was a big waste of time, so companies have incorporated diagnostic and metric systems into their debugging process. Let's define these terms first.

A *diagnostic system* spits out information about what is happening in real time as the tester plays the game. Here's an example of information that is useful for testing sound:

▶ The number of channels playing

▶ A list of sounds playing

▶ The volume of each sound

▶ Specifics of sound interactions (such as whether a texture is assigned properly to trigger the right sound)

Most of these can be found in real-time mixing programs such as Microsoft's Xact (Xbox Audio Content Tool) and Sony's Scream (Scriptable Engine for Audio Manipulation) for PlayStation 2.

Having this kind of information displayed can save programmers an awful lot of time.

A *metric tool* gathers information on the amount of times something occurs and places it into a database. This can be useful if you don't want the player to hear the same piece of music looped 400 times throughout one level. Here are some examples of useful metric data:

▶ The number of times music loops during a level

▶ The number of times a sound effect plays

▶ Whether a sound object is played when no file is associated with it (yes, this happens)

We'll delve more into metric tools in Chapter 7, "Ideal Production."

Cutting Features

At some point in almost every project, there comes a time to eliminate things. It's part of development, but it's also a given that people have a hard time dealing with cuts. Audio features are often cut before other features, because in a cost-benefit analysis they don't stand up as well as other components do. These days, making sure there are shadows in a game will be put ahead of creating an adaptive soundtrack nine times out of ten—and the tenth time, the exception will be made because the game is using that adaptive soundtrack as a basic tenet of the game's design.

It's important to make sure the feature list for the sound engine is prioritized. Such a list prepares you for the worst because you and the programmers agree on what will be cut, and you thus decide what the worst will be before it happens. Here's an example:

1   Sound propagation to the NPC

2   Sound propagation to the listener

3   Acceptable editing/integration system UI for sound team

4   Cross-fading

5   Real-time reverb

6   Adaptive soundtrack

It's also important to keep in mind that when you create this list, you should assume nothing will be cut at all. You should plan realistically. Often there will be a single programmer assigned for audio programming, and he or she will be included only piecemeal on sound. Plan for what is allocated in the programmer schedule—and the earlier you plan how your sound systems will work, the easier it will be to allocate time to those systems before the programmer schedule is finalized.

Understanding Your Platforms

Knowing your hardware means knowing what your limitations are. While this is not the place to discuss platforms in detail, we will take a look at them in brief. (Besides, these machines will be years and years out of date by the time your son or daughter reads this for his or her high school research paper.)

Game Consoles

Microsoft's Xbox is currently at the head of the pack for tech muscle (see **Figure 3.2**). It boasts a hard disk as well as more RAM and, especially, more audio processing than the PlayStation 2 or GameCube has. Its format is 4.3 GB DVD. It also has 64 MB of RAM for use by all systems—sound, art, NPC artificial intelligence code, and so on. However, that doesn't mean it won't compete with a high-end PC that can store over 2 GB of RAM. What's best about the Xbox is that it comes with a powerful tool called XACT (Xbox Audio Creation Tool), which allows programmers and sound designers alike to customize audio in many ways. Let me humor you with a specific: Think about interactive mixing and being able to control the volume of your sounds while playing the game. Top it off with extremely optimized DVD streaming and real-time Dolby Digital capability, and you have a machine that can do some very impressive things for audio.

Sony's PlayStation 2 isn't as phat as Microsoft's Xbox, with only 2 MB of RAM devoted to sound, but it is by no means unimpressive (see **Figure 3.3**). The format is 4.3 GB DVD, just like the Xbox, and folks are squeezing impressive multistreaming out of it. It also featured the very first DTS-based surround game; some might argue that the format is better than Dolby Digital, but most average listeners honestly can't tell the difference. To answer for XACT, Sony (with Buzz Burrowes at Sony Computer Entertainment America) has created the SCREAM

(SCRiptable Engine for Audio Manipulation) tool, which offers similar features for postproduction as well as optimization. We'll delve into these tools in Chapter 7. There's also the little fact that the PS2 is in at least 60 million homes as of this writing, more than three times the scope of the Xbox.

FIGURE 3.2 Microsoft's Xbox offers more RAM and audio processing than the PlayStation 2 or GameCube do.

FIGURE 3.3 Sony's PlayStation 2 accommodates sophisticated multi-streaming as well as DTS sound.

When it comes to tech savvy, the Nintendo GameCube is perhaps the weakest of these three systems, but it does hold a few tricks up its sleeve (see **Figure 3.4**). It doesn't have quite the capacity of DVD on its 3-inch disc, but it does have a custom optical format that holds 1.5 GB, along with an impressive 40 MB of RAM compared with the PlayStation2's 32 MB. It has comparable capability for streaming, if your programmer puts in a few hours of overtime. It also was the first console to feature Dolby Pro Logic II, which was designed to offer effects similar to Dolby Digital's without discrete channel panning. Factor 5, a team LucasArts plucked from Germany and brought to California, worked on the sound system for GameCube and got quite a lot of punch for the audio in *Star Wars Rogue Squadron,* which was one of the first *Star Wars* games to create a feel awfully close to that of the Death Star assault, for sound as well as the visuals.

FIGURE 3.4 Nintendo's GameCube was the first console to feature Dolby Pro Logic II.

Handheld and Portable Devices

Handheld devices from PalmPilots to cell phones have the widest variety of sound hardware of late. Some of these portable marvels of technology can play back 16 channels of MIDI-controlled instruments. Some play back digital samples. Many of them have their own development kits, but not all of those kits are well tailored for creating audio. Still, with such small devices producing such impressive audio, we must pause to say "Wow." Once again we will not include all the specifics, because if we did so this would be a whole different kind of book. However, consider a few pointers about handheld and portable devices:

First of all, if you're developing audio for a handheld or portable, don't get too caught up with one development kit; many are out there and many more will appear over the years. Familiarize yourself first with minute limitations (small amounts of RAM, for example) and primitive compositional tools such as step-time composition and tracking. This will prepare you to learn a new platform in a day or two, so that you can start producing audio right away.

Handheld devices are usually at least two generations behind the current state-of-the-art. The latest Nintendo portable, the Game Boy Advance, matches or exceeds the quality of the Super Nintendo, which is two generations behind the Nintendo GameCube. This means that if you've already developed on these systems, learning the technology restrictions of handheld audio will be a breeze.

The PC

The PC is another rapidly evolving platform. Compared with consoles, the PC has technology that revolves around more basic parameters such as the following limitations:

▶ Operating system: A PC is only as good as the operating system it uses, because this is what you use to access the hardware. In some cases, developers can bypass the operating system, but this is happening more rarely now because doing so greatly lengthens development time.

▶ Bus speed: This is how fast data can be transported, whether from RAM, a hard drive, or an expansion card. If your bus can transport 128 bits of data simultaneously, you have a tremendous advantage over 32-bit bus systems.

▶ RAM: The current limitation for RAM on PCs is around 4 GB. Audio folk are nearly past the point where they need to fight for RAM, unless they're doing a cross-platform title and need to adhere to the PC limitations of the least powerful platform.

▶ Storage: When the CD-ROM became widely used as a storage medium, game audio changed forever. When compression emerged, it changed again, because the amount of audio that could be stored increased exponentially. However, on a PC, where hard drives start in the 40 GB range and games size up to be no more than 5 GB each on average, music and voice are having a hard time filling this space (provided compression is used, and it almost always is).

▶ Dedicated hardware: PCs are far more expandable than consoles, and this expandability is their biggest strength. To compete with console and arcade quality in the mid-1990s, dedicated graphics hardware emerged and provided PC users with an even more incredible graphics experience than anything consoles could offer at the time. These days one company has a stranglehold on the sound card market—Creative (formerly Creative Labs, the maker of the illustrious Sound Blaster line)—and it's pushing audio acceleration just as 3dfx pushed graphic acceleration. It's possible to create great game audio without custom chip sets; just check out what's being done to push the envelope for PCs and whether it will be worth your while to support it.

These five areas are important to keep in mind during audio development for PC games. Also keep in mind that developing exclusively for the PC is a risky proposition if you are spending a lot of money on your game's development. Simultaneous platform release is a hallmark of the largest game publishers.

Working with Programmers

Programmers are your friends. They are in fact the ones who will determine whether you are happy or sad about how your sounds play back in the game, so treat them with respect. Having said that, programmers are not necessarily audio savvy. It's up to you to show them the cost-benefit analyses and the virtues of well-done audio along the way so they understand your viewpoints.

Communication

To begin with, know how to communicate. Do *not* be afraid to use extremely simple language and syntax. For example, if you tell a programmer, "I want this 3D sound to have a controllable falloff curve," that won't explain that "the player needs to hear an impact sound even if it is far away, to demonstrate that the sound is realistic—so as the missile is flying away, we should fade it quickly at first, and more slowly the farther away it gets." Just because programmers are engineers doesn't mean they can read your mind. This sort of thing seems like common sense, but you'd be surprised by how many people assume that any person's knowledge base is the same as their own.

Another great method of communication is demonstrating issues rather than discussing them. For instance, it's far easier to draw diagrams of how sound is defined in a level of the game and actually demonstrate bugs to coders in person than it is to explain these problems in multiple e-mails.

Finally, prioritize your issues. Having a bug database is very useful for this. For example, if you're having a problem with how reverb is affecting sound in a particular level, don't designate it with a priority higher than that of a problem you're having with the sound in a particular level not playing at all. You need the producers, QA staff, and whoever is running the bug database to trust your judgment.

File management

First, make sure that your assets are inside a file-management system of some kind. A system such as NXN Alienbrain is an excellent example. The directory structure for your assets can appear on your local drive exactly as it does in the file manager. When a file needs to be edited, only one person at a time can edit it. New techniques are allowing files to be edited by multiple people, but that requires more workflow management, as simultaneous file editing is one of the easiest ways to make a game break.

System sharing

System data can be shared to the audio engine's advantage. Let's say you plan to piggyback your sound-field map display on top of the collision system (which governs the boundaries of objects such that if the boundaries touch, the objects behave in an appropriate manner). This means you will use the same display for how sound is represented in various areas of level geometry as the system that dictates what surfaces are defined for collision. Usually this is a good way to do things, as you can save considerable processor time by describing sound data in a more abstract—and simplified—sense than the way it is actually displayed. For example, a sound can bounce off a rectangular pillar almost as convincingly as it bounces off a cylindrical pillar, and the rectangular pillar takes far less polygons.

It's important to realize that while the sound might be using the same data the collision system is, the way the data is displayed must be kept separate during editing. To do this, a good sound designer or engineer will request a special sound-field edit mode, during which all that is needed is to insert ambient sounds and change parameters. A collision edit mode, on the other hand, may allow a level designer to actually move and tweak the geometry of the level itself. These specialized modes keep the sound editors from inadvertently making changes to work designers have made on actual level geometry. A designer doesn't want an audio developer to change a staircase from straight to circular, and an audio developer doesn't want a designer to turn bird chirps into house music.

System Responsibility

You would think that each system that interfaces with audio would have a designated programmer to whom you could go in the event of a problem. This is not always the case, so it is very important to keep track of who is responsible for what at all times. But wait, the sound engine should take care of all that, right? Strictly speaking, the sound engine in a game will not perform all the functions required to make sounds trigger. At its root, a sound engine is a tool for playback only, not necessarily something tailored to game-specific behavior. Let's look at an example. Programmer x may be responsible for weapon behavior, including how weapons sound when they are fired. Right when he's in the middle of working on this code, he might be called upon to work on a more important system such as rendering. In such a situation, it's up to the audio director to either reschedule implementation plans or figure out who will be taking over weapon code.

Once technology has been tackled and you have a plan in place to build a system that is both organized and efficient, you can begin to figure out how to design the game itself. We'll take a look at this in the next chapter.

CHAPTER 4
Design

"DESIGN RULES ALL." This has been declared upon the founding of more than one game development house. Over the years, game design has increased in complexity by such an order of magnitude that many seasoned game designers at the larger publishers have left to start smaller development teams. These designers can certainly handle larger projects, but they find simplicity in game design increasingly appealing given the trend toward complexity.

Game audio has been increasing in complexity as well. For example, a physics system, which allows objects to make the correct sounds when they strike or scrape different surfaces, is transparent to the average player, but the technology needed to make that engine work is on the cutting edge of game audio and requires large chunks of development time and resources. Ion Storm's *Deus Ex: Invisible War* is one of the first titles to use a fully featured physics sound system (**Figure 4.1**).

FIGURE 4.1 Games such as Ion Storm's *Deus Ex: Invisible War* utilize physics system technology that is transparent to the player but difficult for audio developers to achieve.

In fact, audio has come such a long way that it's influencing the way games are designed rather than the other way around. Exemplifying this trend are Sony's *Parappa the Rapper* and Sega's *Rez*, in which music is the most influential part of the game's design.

In this chapter, I explore how design influences audio and vice versa. I begin by discussing one of the most exciting topics in the linking of audio design and game design: *adaptive audio*. Many people consider this area of game design too arcane to bother with, when in fact it has been in use for many years and is at the heart of what makes game audio unique.

Adaptive Audio

Adaptive audio has been defined and redefined many times since game audio began; currently it is understood as any audio that is nonlinear or nonreactive in a game. For example, in a linear medium such as a cut scene, a movie, or a full-motion video clip, the audio is linear: It doesn't change no matter how many times the medium is played. The same is true when someone is playing a level of a game with a looped piece of music. If the player presses a button and something happens either through sound effects or music, the audio is reactive; however, if the player's actions cause a number of different transitions in the soundtrack, the audio can be classified as adaptive on the game design side, since the game itself is changing based on the player's actions. Taking it yet another step further, if the audio influences the player's choices, the audio can be classified as adaptive—but on the player side. When the previously mentioned transitions take place, the soundtrack or sound effects "adapt" to a player's gameplay choices and in turn match or enhance the experience.

What makes videogames different from movies is that in a game, a player influences the outcome, which can be different each time the game is played. This is the first thing every composer needs to know when creating music for a game. Without this knowledge, a composer assumes that the game experience will be linear and thus creates only one piece of music for any given situation, rather than several pieces or several variations on a piece. It's not just about getting your hands on a live orchestra; it's about creating an entirely new means of musical expression. So why is music more important than sound for adaptive audio?

For the most part, music is what drives adaptive audio, since music is more abstract than sound and can be less attached to the visuals. For example, a game's depiction of an explosion should have some sort of sound associated with it to indicate that there is an explosion going on. Music does not have this sort of requirement.

No bones about it, creating an adaptive audio soundtrack is hard. Few people have done it well. This is because most uninitiated game composers consider adaptive audio as daunting as any kind of programming. Even some hardened veterans refuse to delve into it because it is so far removed from writing music and creating sound effects. Even fewer have done it so well that they are known for it. I will present just a few of the souls worthy of mention who have contributed adaptive and dynamic soundtracks to games.

NOTE The examples I give in this chapter are almost exclusively PC games. This is not because console games haven't used adaptive soundtracks, but because I haven't experienced any of them. With apologies to the console crowd, I've heard whispers of such console games, but the people I talk to about adaptive audio are primarily PC developers. I encourage everyone in the audio community to add to your store of knowledge about adaptive soundtrack usage by going to `www.adaptiveaudio.org` (Figure 4.2).

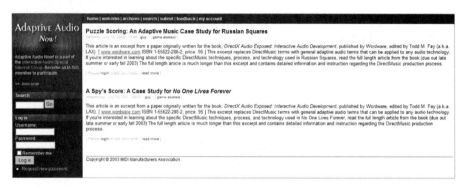

FIGURE 4.2 Adaptive Audio Now is an initiative started by Guy Whitmore for professionals and amateurs alike to post tales of their adaptive-audio techniques. Check it out at `www.adaptiveaudio.org`.

LucasArts and iMUSE

LucasArts has made some of the best computer games ever, and part of the company's greatness comes from its advanced and groundbreaking approach to audio. You can find a fantastic history of LucasArts on the company's Web site, `www.lucasarts.com/20th/history_1.htm`, but how inconsiderate of me to tempt those nestled in bed with this book to reach over to their laptop to read it. To sum it up, the founding members of LucasArts had state-of-the-art games in mind when they began the company in 1983, but they took sound more seriously than most in the industry did. Indeed, they hired some very imaginative folks, among them Michael Land (LucasArts' audio director), Peter McConnell, and Clint Bajakian—the triumvirate behind the musical magic in LucasArts games.

In the late 1980s, Michael spearheaded an effort to create something called the Interactive Music Streaming Engine—hence the name iMUSE. Essentially this was an engine that handled first MIDI tracks and later digital audio tracks, and enabled the MIDI tracks to branch and loop. This was the first time this sort of endeavor had been pursued in earnest; more than $1 million was spent on its development over a period of ten years, and the company applied for a patent. It's also the only interactive-adaptive music system that has its own fan site: `http://imuse.mixnmojo.com/what.shtml`.

The iMUSE engine was designed specifically for the kind of games that LucasArts developed, which at the time were mostly graphic adventures. The company is still most renowned for its adventure games, the latest and greatest being *Knights of the Old Republic.* Back in the old days, a graphic adventure consisted of a character wandering through environments that took up a whole screen at a time. When the character wandered toward the edge of the screen, the scene cut to the next place they were going. The game's design could be mapped on a flowchart fairly easily, and the musicians were able to create music based on the chart. This is perhaps the ultimate example of a development process map (DPM) driving the design of the game as well as the music composition.

The first title to use iMUSE was *Monkey Island 2: LeChuck's Revenge* (**Figure 4.3**), released in 1991. LucasArts' audio team used the system to allow different tracks (either single MIDI instruments or sets of them, depending on the situation) to be introduced and then removed as the player moved from place to place within the same screen, not just from screen to screen. Thus sometimes the music shifted when the player moved to a different room in the same screen.

FIGURE 4.3 *Monkey Island 2: LeChuck's Revenge* was the first title to use the iMUSE sound engine.

Later, iMUSE was used with great success with streamed stereo audio files in *The Dig,* another LucasArts classic. Many people thought they were forward-thinking when they claimed that a soundtrack might one day have a sweeping orchestral score. Well, they had no idea: *The Dig* presented an incredible orchestral score by Michael Land, with plenty of dynamics and an almost exclusive use of Wagnerian strings. The LucasArts team licensed recordings of Wagner, then cut them up and used them in conjunction with synthesized samples of other instruments. The occasional solo live instrument was recorded in-house at LucasArts to complete the soundtrack. The clever use of cross-fading made a soundtrack composed in pieces sound seamless.

The original LucasArts music team is pursuing other interests now, but its legacy lives on in the eight or so major LucasArts titles that used iMUSE. The engine will take its place in videogame music history, as it had a hand in perhaps the greatest adaptive soundtracks of its time.

3D First-Person Adaptive Soundtracks

Nearly every game uses three-dimensional sound in some form or another nowadays, but with the remake of *Castle Wolfenstein* in 1990 a whole new game genre was born: *3D FP*, or 3D first-person. People were now seeing the screen as though they were in the adventure looking through the eyes of the player character.

In 1992, the first major title to use an interactive soundtrack with a first-person perspective was the Looking Glass/Origin collaboration *Ultima Underworld: The Stygian Abyss* (**Figure 4.4**).

FIGURE 4.4 Ultima Underworld: The Stygian Abyss provided a truly enriching experience in 3D first-person, with an adaptive soundtrack to boot.

George Sanger (aka The Fatman) and Dave Govett created a number of pieces related to the player's actions, from wandering to fighting. The music shifted based on variables such as an enemy attacking the player (not just being within sight of the player, mind you).

Unfortunately, this title was produced during a transitional period in game instrumentation. Small sets of samples were built into sound cards (such sets came to be known as *General MIDI,* since the sets were supposed to be the same on all sound cards) and triggered by MIDI commands; they were expertly crafted so that if you concentrated you could hear a full, beautiful orchestral score. These days you don't have to concentrate to hear the richness of the music, so let's give credit where credit is due: to the pioneers.

In 1995, another 3D FP game with an adaptive soundtrack was released: Delphine Software's *Fade to Black.* In theory, this title should have taken adaptive audio a step further, as it was released three years later, but it didn't. Instead, its music switched in a split second from a tense, ambient General MIDI track to a pulse-pounding timpani, regardless of whether you could see an enemy nearby. If the enemy was behind you on a catwalk, the music tipped you off. This was a failure on the part of the adaptive track, as it unnecessarily influenced players with something completely outside the playing environment. This isn't to say the music itself was bad, but the way it was integrated screwed up the overall immersiveness of the game.

Another 3D FP game, *Unreal* by Epic Megagames (now Epic Games), used MOD files, so called because the first music files used the .mod extension in their filenames. These are not General MIDI files; rather, they use whatever samples the composer chooses, up to a certain size limit per file. For *Unreal* the MOD file size limit was 1 MB. Considering that the sound bank for General MIDI on sound cards at the time (the SoundBlaster AWE32 and AWE64, circa 1997) was only 1 MB, *Unreal* was able to have truly unique and high-quality sound. MOD files could also be manipulated more than MIDI files could: By simply typing a number, you could tweak vibrato for each time subdivision, whether it was an eighth note or a sixty-fourth note. It sounds programmer-centric, but MODs exploded in the PC music scene around 1993 and haven't stopped since.

With the MOD file format, the composers at Straylight Productions were able to loop sections of music devoted to as many gameplay situations as were needed, from suspense to action to death to exploration. They could also create various fade (not cross-fade) settings so that music transitions would be smoother.

Still, even with the more advanced techniques used in *Unreal* and other games like it, the audio wasn't nearly as convincing as that of a film when it came to smooth transitions, good modulation, and emotional impact. The quality of MOD files still paled in comparison with a live score, and the audio transitions based on combat or exploration were getting old. It would take better techniques and another four years before orchestras and exponentially larger orchestral samples would allow game composers to create a more dramatic and powerful sonic landscape using a soundtrack.

The audio folks behind *Deus Ex: Invisible War* used a different technique. As the audio director of this project, I arranged for various areas in the game to change instrumentation or change the soundtrack completely, using cross-fades for the environment. This capability was always there in conjunction with newly available ambient sound effects. Ambient sound effects made an overwhelming impact in the title *Thief* in 1998 (**Figure 4.5**)—and in a subtler way much earlier, in 1989, with the Amiga title *Dungeon Master*, influencing players to make major gameplay decisions based on ambient sounds alone for the first time. In addition to the ambience and varied environmental music, triggers based on various situations could either switch the entire soundtrack or play a one-shot piece of music. It was very dynamic but not used in nearly enough places, so the soundtrack ended up being mostly ambient, while it could have been far more expressive. Yep, I blame myself.

FIGURE 4.5 *Thief* may not have been a looker graphically, but its alternative stealth gameplay and stunningly atmospheric sound put it in a class of its own.

Remember the ambient sound I mentioned earlier? And how *Thief* blew the doors off the competition with this kind of sound? Nowadays, people like Erik Kraber at Electronic Arts are jumping on the "hard work on sound effects makes a better game" bandwagon with painfully serious, top-notch sound design and mixing work. Let's explore a bit more of what's going on in the increasingly complex realm of game audio.

Interactive Mixing and Dynamic Range

Currently the two major areas of interest in game audio are interactive mixing and dynamic range.

Interactive Mixing

Interactive mixing—that is, mixing game-audio content while the game is playing as part of the final stage of sound engineering—is a relatively new concept, but it's a process audio developers have wanted for a long time. Without interactive mixing, making a change to a sound's volume, for example, required changing code or text outside the game 99 percent of the time. This meant you had to tweak the sound separately and then test it within the game over and over until you got it right, a process that seemed interminable.

Now we have the means for audio folk to change any number of parameters in real time. Microsoft's Xact (Xbox Audio Content Tool) and Sony's Scream (Scriptable Engine for Audio Manipulation) mixing programs do this, and so does Renderware Studio by Criterion, a commercially available game-sound engine for multiple platforms. Eventually mixing and mastering a game will become a job separate enough to warrant hiring someone specialized for the task. This will happen within the next few years. Let's take a look ahead at what the specialized job will entail.

Ideally, the sound designer will load the game and look at a master list to see what sounds are playing. Indicators include volume bars in the form of decibel meters, one for each sound playing, that flash in the control software or level editor (such as Renderware Studio—or, in the case of the Unreal engine, UnrealEd). These days, many systems still superimpose a text list over the game, forcing the designer to scan the list quickly to see the names, some of which pop up for just milliseconds at a time. (Let that be a nudge to the tool developers out there.)

When the sounds need to be mixed so that one effect doesn't overpower others, you can turn down a sound's volume with the twist of a knob or the movement of an onscreen fader. You can also use faders for equalizing, filtering, and adding effects to the sounds. If your programmer has time to code these controls, definitely make use of him. It'll be well worth the integration time.

While you mix audio, remember to base your judgment on a sound that occurs throughout the game on its global use as well as its local use. This means that if a machine gun sounds too loud at a relatively soft level, don't turn it down if it's likely to get drowned at a level with higher volume or more range. If necessary, create a customized sound object for that level and adjust the volume only for that object rather than changing the sound globally. Now that I've mentioned the words *global*, *local*, and *range*, it's a nice opportunity to enter the next section.

Dynamic Range

Dynamic range is becoming increasingly important in audio development because it deals with overall volume considerations. Ever wonder why television commercials are always louder than the program you're watching? It's deliberate—the advertisers want your attention—but that doesn't stop the experience from being annoying. Films avoid this sort of jarring volume change unless they intentionally use it as a plot device. The same applies to game audio. The difference in volume is described technically as dynamic range.

Unfortunately, dynamic range can't be fixed during gameplay without the help of a real-time dynamics process such as a compressor. This is a consideration that sound designers must incorporate from the beginning. A lot of developers use their highest volume in the game as the same volume played when they turn on a console and the console logo is played. Most consoles have a company or console logo introduction with a volume that rivals that of the THX logo in movies— that would be the maximum volume, and it's usually a good starting point. From there, you need to figure out how voice, sound effects, and music will all interact.

In games, a good way to let players set their own preferences is to give them an options screen with a fader control (**Figure 4.6**) that will act as a volume control for an entire sound set. Such functionality has been available for a long time, but it doesn't help if an individual sound file is already so loud it would break an eardrum.

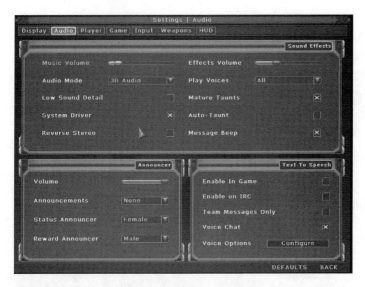

FIGURE 4.6 The user-controlled dynamic range in *Unreal Tournament 2004* includes an options screen and volume sliders. Players should have to use these as little as possible.

Beyond setting the game's maximum volume, you can get good dynamic range by using several other techniques. The most obvious (and tedious) of these is doing a good solid interactive mixing pass before the game ships. This involves, yep, playing the *entire game* and correcting any sounds or music that are too loud or too soft, fixing equalization and effects, and so on—polishing whatever audio needs it.

Another method, which can be used in conjunction with the overall audio pass, is setting appropriate ranges in each sound category. Todd Simmons, a sound designer at Ion Storm, suggested this idea while we worked on *Deus Ex: Invisible War,* and it's brilliant: Set levels for voice at the highest range—from, say, –13 dB to –6 dB RMS. The RMS, or root mean square function, is a way of maximizing the sound level (also known as *normalizing*) across the entire waveform rather than maximizing the peaks. Don't worry about what RMS means technically; just know that it's an option in programs such as Sound Forge (**Figure 4.7**). You'll find the RMS option in the Normalize function.

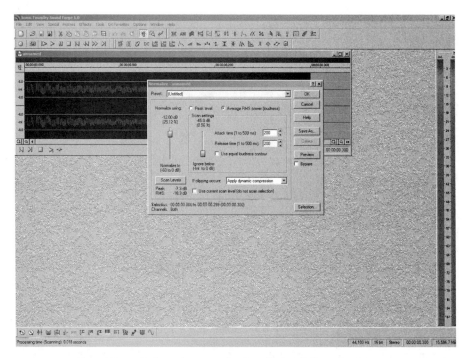

FIGURE 4.7 Sound Forge 6 allows for normalization via the RMS option. You can scan levels to see what the average decibel and peak decibel levels are.

We set voice for the highest levels, because voice is the most important sound in the game that needs to be heard clearly. This is a standard rule in film audio as well. Next, we set levels for sound effects as the second-highest category of normalized sounds, at −18 dB to −13 dB RMS. Sounds are almost as important as voice in terms of being heard clearly by the player, as they are vital for player feedback. Music is usually normalized at the lowest levels (the levels used on *Deus Ex: Invisible War* were −25 dB to −18 dB RMS or so), but these can vary depending on how they are used. If you want to use a piece of music to frighten the player with a quick staccato cacophony of instruments, for example, the normalization should be much higher than −25 dB RMS. Figure 4.7 shows Sound Forge's "average dB RMS" function at work.

3D propagation and falloff curves

While you can align your sounds perfectly for volume based on straight playback, your sound requirements change in a game in which distance is a factor—a common element in games with a first-person perspective. As if changing in distance relative to the listener, a sound's volume will change accordingly. Falloff curves are important to consider here: They describe how an object's sound will change as its distance from the player changes.

Say you have a sound for which you want to gain a certain amount of volume until it reaches its maximum (the average db RMS range discussed above). This could mean that some softer sounds will fall off too quickly if they're not as loud as others initially. For example, if you need footsteps to be audible while guards are shooting pistols, the pistol sound might be jacked up quite a bit while the footsteps get lost in the mix. You can change your falloff curve to reflect this so that the pistol sounds reach their maximum levels sooner than the footstep sounds do based on distance. Check out the chart in **Figure 4.8**. The curves represent exponential curves and linear curves, all of which are adjustable.

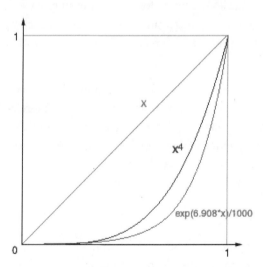

FIGURE 4.8 Distance falloff curves, from linear to exponential. An exponential curve is more commonly used, as it represents a smoother volume change to the average listener. For easier mixing later on, keep these curves adjustable based on either sound groups or even individual sounds.

You can use another option in place of or in conjunction with the falloff curve method: sound radii. In certain game engines such as Unreal, the developer has control over the radius in which a sound can be heard. Some engines have two radii, one representing the point at which the sound volume drops to zero, and the other representing the point at which the sound reaches maximum volume (the point at which it is normalized) in relation to the player. Increasing the radius for maximum volume would make the footsteps more audible, as they would hold their volume for a longer period of time depending on the player's movement in combat.

Music for Different Game Types

Once you have a good grasp of the design you want to implement, you can start thinking about more creative aspects of audio development. I begin by citing some excellent examples of how music is being used in different ways for various game types.

Music for games used to have a single development strategy: Learn the technology and be its slave, but coax impressive things out of it. If you reach the level where people can hear it and say, "That's kinda cool," you've won the battle.

Now that the CD-ROM drive enables audio to stream for games, the rules have changed. You can use any means necessary to create music, because the music can be as similar to (or as different from) any other music written before—without the technological constraints.

This advance, coupled with the fact that videogames are making more money than the record and film industries combined, has lured many a fresh thinker (or money-grubber, to some) into the game-audio arena, searching for new outlets now possible with the most rapidly evolving entertainment delivery system in history. Thus more and more people are coming up with new ways—some interesting and some disastrous—of creating game audio. I'll focus on the interesting stuff.

Music Licensing

Music licensing has taken the game-music world by storm. Two major publishers now include a job title of music executive: the person responsible for placing music that will add to a game's selling power. Interestingly enough, these same people aren't as interested in adaptive technique as they are in licensing, mostly because licensing is an avenue that can create millions in cross-promotional dollars. In some cases the decisions these executives make are sheer genius. Let's take a look at one of the crown jewels of music licensing: *Wipeout XL.*

Wipeout XL, developed by Psygnosis, was among the first games to successfully use licensing in a major way, back in 1997. The title is a racing-car game set in the future where advanced hover cars go at insane speeds. The game is filled with metal, concrete, and explosions. As such, some bright spark at Psygnosis decided to link the game with popular electronica pieces of the age from bands such as The Future Sound of London, Underworld, Orbital, Daft Punk, and Prodigy. The music fit the game like a glove. The in-house composer, Tim Wright, even wrote a few songs alongside the pop artists, and it all blended together seamlessly. It was a dream come true, a marriage of game audio and popular style, wrapped up in a neat and polished package that even sold quite a few copies of a separate soundtrack. From that, there was only one step to a full orchestra in a game.

Live Orchestra

I use the term *live orchestra* loosely, to mean there are composers who have written tracks—by using massive sample libraries and a bit of midnight tweaking—that most listeners can't distinguish from live music.

The earliest game I can remember that used live musicians in an orchestra probably isn't the first such game, but I must mention it. *Total Annihilation*, released in 1997, was a futuristic strategy title for the PC that featured some impressive live orchestral work by the Seattle Northwest Sinfonia, written by Jeremy Soule. Soule got his start in 1995 doing a very good soundtrack for *Secret of Evermore* for the Super Nintendo. The soundtrack was so damned good that no one could ignore its impact. It could have been any game type, and the music would have gotten the same attention.

However, now that the way for live orchestra has been paved, the challenge for videogame composers who swear by live orchestras is to create music that rivals that of the film composers who swear by it. After all, more and more reviews are comparing game soundtracks to those of television and film. But hey, we don't need that. We got our own juice.

The message I'm sending here is that the orchestra is a tool. It can be used just like any other tool. The fact that it generates emotion easily just makes it more seductive to plunk down with Gigastudio and play a few chords, but don't discount the other tools in the box.

Guy Whitmore and Russian Squares

Let's take a look in the other direction, away from the cameras and the lights, the tuxes, and the champagne during intermission. Here is probably the best-documented case of adaptive audio (see `www.adaptiveaudio.org` and search for `Russian Squares`), with music quality that rivals what you'd expect to pick up at the store under "Electronica."

For the puzzle game *Russian Squares,* audio composer Guy Whitmore ignored the orchestra and instead constructed music using an advanced form of MOD: a DLS2 sample set. Downloadable Sounds (DLS) is a standard developed by the Interactive Audio Special Interest Group (IASIG) to combat the problem presented by General MIDI that we explored earlier in this chapter and that has already been well documented. The result of Guy's and the other composers' work on *Russian Squares* is something that smacks of resounding quality and, best of all, changes and morphs the music completely but subtly. For almost every action in the game, Guy created a musical transition that could change the music state. For example, in the piece "GravityRide" there are 28 different music *cells.* Each cell consists of any number of changes, from a new beat to the addition of a new instrument, to the tempo or meter changing in an existing beat or instrument. Even the latest Web-based and wildly popular Pop Cap games can't boast that.

I've explored at least a few of the ways that game design and music can intertwine successfully. Up to this point, I've covered the bases of workflow, technology, and design. In the next chapter, I turn to a real test case, *Deus Ex: Invisible War,* in which I examine all three more closely.

CHAPTER 5
Audio Integration: Postmortem

DEUS EX: INVISIBLE WAR, developed by Ion Storm and published by Eidos Interactive, was released in the summer of 2003 on the Microsoft Xbox and PC platforms. This title is an excellent example of game development that used advanced technology and rigorous production standards. The process of creating *DE:IW* also reveals some of the challenges of integrating audio with the rest of the game. I will describe this aspect of *DE:IW*'s development.

The team that developed *DE:IW* was thrown together for the first time and employed a lot of creative innovation, more so than with any other project I've worked on. However, the team also went through major growing pains and thus learned many lessons about proper management and workflow the hard way— after problems arose. My synopsis focuses more on procedure than on personal interaction. Keep in mind, though, that the latter is important, and take into account the lessons discussed in earlier chapters about communication, semantics, and familiarity with other perspectives and paradigms.

DE:IW is referred to most often as an action role-playing game. In truth, it has elements of many different gameplay types. The action is set in a postapocalyptic future with conspiracies, factions, and human-body augmentation running rampant (**Figure 5.1**). The player receives goals and can choose a number of ways to achieve them, from violence to espionage. For example, if a door with a guard presents an obstacle, the player can shoot the guard and blow up the door, or stun the guard unconscious and pick the door's lock, or search the area for ventilation shafts and crawl around the door.

Billie Adams: The only safe way to deal with such dangerous power in such an unstable individual is to destroy him. It's the only way.

FIGURE 5.1 Deus Ex: Invisible War and its predecessor, Deus Ex, have been paving the way for new modes of experiencing an adventure or role-playing game.

This style of gameplay in a first-person game is called an *immersive simulation.* The term might sound redundant, but there are also nonimmersive simulations, such as flight simulators. Going a step beyond the simple videogame mechanics we'd grown used to, immersive simulation provides a unique approach to presenting audio. With immersive simulation as the foundation of the *Deus Ex* series, *DE:IW* was created to make the player feel as though he were actually in the game environment, by means of realistic elements such as surround sound and audio effects of higher quality than those of previous games.

Workflow Report

The most valuable lesson I learned on the *DE:IW* audio team was that a solid schedule and regular communication are vital to the proper coordination of resources. Let's begin with preproduction.

Preproduction and Studio Construction

DE:IW preproduction took place at the same time as the "port" of the original *Deus Ex* to the Sony PlayStation 2 platform, as well as plans for a sequel to the *Thief* series. The audio team consisted of one audio director (myself) and an intern who handled a good deal of sound-file conversion for the *Deus Ex* port.

Preproduction involved making decisions about platforms, basic gameplay, and art concepts. We also began discussing the audio engine shortly after starting the project, even though audio production didn't become a factor until much later. We decided to go with the Xbox and PC platforms; the game had to be cutting-edge, and these had the most advanced technology available to handle the significant demands that the gameplay and art concepts were demonstrating. This would work in audio's favor, of course, because Xbox and PC had good audio-rendering capabilities as well. This was a bold decision, since the PlayStation2 captured a greater percentage of the market, but the team wasn't interested in pandering to the market as much as it was in creating the newest and most enjoyable experience it could based on the groundbreaking standards that *Deus Ex* set.

During preproduction, the audio department made plans for a voice recording studio, as the development company was moving to a new facility. After three budgets were drawn up and reviewed, the studio director, Warren Spector, chose the one with moderate expense and the greatest bang for the buck. As the audio director, I generated an audio intranet site showing sample sounds, and I started a rudimentary task-reporting system. I also instituted "Field and Foley Day" on which to record custom sound effects.

Design Discussions and Scheduling

The most difficult challenges were that (1) we didn't have a full team until mid-way through preproduction; (2) it was the first time the team had worked with consoles as opposed to PCs; and (3) *DE:IW* was probably the most complex and ambitious game that had ever been attempted. Thus, because of the piecemeal nature of the team and the fact that another game was being developed at the same time as *DE:IW,* communication between management and the team likewise was piecemeal and irregular until production was well under way. Most of the communication involved design discussions.

A criterion the audio leads did establish for design was that music would not be in the forefront of the audio mix. The game was to be as immersive as possible. Music that was too loud or thematic would create a jarring effect. The team's project director, Harvey Smith, cited the *Thief* series as an example to follow. We also established that sound would be instrumental for the nonplayer characters (NPCs) to use as a gameplay function. For example, guards could hear the player and respond to his movement or actions, and the player in turn could either sneak or move slowly, or activate an augmentation in his biomodified body that would allow him to move silently at higher speeds.

For scheduling, having a brilliant team was only the starting point. Managing a brilliant team proves more difficult than managing a somewhat less brilliant one. The team's top decision makers were all such strong-willed, outspoken intellectuals that enforcing a nonunanimous decision was difficult without some management muscle. That muscle wasn't available because studio director Warren Spector didn't want to put too much pressure on the leads; in the past, that approach had put a clamp on creativity—with devastating results. Warren had been the project director on the original *Deus Ex* and was familiar with draconian management styles, which he had fought and which had caused team morale to deteriorate. Unfortunately, this caution led to a decision-by-committee structure in which the leads were to be self-managing without any external influence. This created a number of issues. The key was to find a compromise between establishing a schedule and fostering creative freedom—fundamentally the biggest challenge any game team faces and a problem that grows with the complexity of a project. The compromises in this project came to be known as "straw men."

A straw man argument is one too weak in substance to be legitimately backed up. Such an argument usually is made with the intention of helping a project, when in fact it has not been thought out well enough to be helpful; instead it becomes detrimental. During the development of *DE:IW,* most of the solutions proposed as alternatives to management's initial plans were straw men mostly because the technology and design were new and untested. It was also hard to accurately estimate the time these alternative solutions would take. For example, one proposal was to use reverb (the echo of sounds at various levels in the game) in hardware: Instead of code being written by programmers and processed through a CPU, a custom chip with built-in reverb would be used to process the echo of sounds at various levels. This idea was eventually given up because programmers didn't have the time to implement any kind of reverb. It was considered a lower priority than a system that would allow more optimized loading of files from the game DVD.

The audio team was not above using straw man arguments. One of the producers initially proposed that three months would be enough time to program an audio engine in conjunction with our existing code. The audio team contested this, but because we were dealing with new technology, we couldn't provide enough concrete examples or alternatives to refute it. The audio staff also wanted reverb to be generated in code rather than built into the files, but again couldn't present enough reason to warrant the request. The team's lack of intellectual assertiveness was a detriment. Management used straw men successfully as a means to drive the project forward during the latter half of the schedule—and to push the team to deliver a gold master by the deadline defined in the milestone description, which had been mutually agreed on by Ion and Eidos.

Interfacing with the Audio Team

Assumption is the mother of false information. I learned this the hard way on *DE:IW.* Programmers assigned to a particular segment of the game code don't automatically think about what's necessary for audio. They also don't automatically think that they need to consult the audio team during the preproduction process. It's up to the audio team lead to interface with the programmer lead in order to define and mutually agree on specifications for any part of the audio that might involve a programmer.

The same is true of art and animation: Do not assume that an artist creating a crate will understand how the physical attributes of the crate will affect sound. And don't assume a texture artist will follow a file-naming convention in accordance with a physics engine that uses sound files to match surface assignments (more on this later).

By the same token, management should not assume that the audio folks are aware of all matters that might affect them. While the audio leads are responsible for finding out, producers are also responsible for making sure information is available as soon as possible, to avoid redundant or unusable work.

All of these assumptions were made in some form or another during the development of *DE:IW*. What will keep them from happening for you is communicating clearly as well as keeping informed of decisions and following them.

Let's take a look at how the value of audio to an entire game team is reflected in the audio staff's size. A team of five composers contributed to the sound and music of *Unreal*, a game released six years earlier with similar asset production requirements as those of *DE:IW*. The sound team of *DE:IW* consisted of three people, only one of whom was present for the entirety of development. Moreover, there were three artists on *Unreal* and 14 on *DE:IW*. There were 14 artists on *Unreal 2* as well, and more than 15 people are credited with sound work on that title.

Technology Report

We've covered the importance of technology. It's really important. Really, *really* important. This was something that the audio team was fortunate enough to handle well, for the most part. The sound programmer, Brian Sharp, who in the past had worked mostly with rendering code, was enthusiastic about the work and very helpful in providing team members with the tools they needed to implement audio effectively.

Building the Engine

The details of the audio engine Ion Storm used in *DE:IW* as well as in *Thief: Deadly Shadows* are of course confidential (with the exception of the physics engine, which was discussed at Game Developers Conference 2004). It's also an extremely advanced engine, and while I would love to discuss the details, that would be like discussing the code base of the iMUSE engine that LucasArts built: absolute sacrilege—since iMUSE is still regarded as a magical adaptive music system—and also illegal. However, I am free to divulge the building process on a conceptual level, as this does not constitute copyrightable intellectual property.

Construction time

As I mentioned earlier, the *DE:IW* audio engine was scheduled to take three months to build. It was even said that an initial version would be available after only two months once construction of the audio engine began. Neither of these estimates was accurate; it actually took around five months. It took this long because a number of reassignments had to make room for higher-priority code work, such as DVD streaming and an object property system (which would allow the design team to create playable levels). All this had to be done by one programmer. A lesson from this? The audio staff needs to be flexible and able to reevaluate task completion based on the engine's staggered construction schedule. But a more important lesson involved the proper scheduling and management of programming tasks, which I will discuss in Chapter 7, "Ideal Production."

Feature set

The feature set for the *DE:IW* engine was designed around functions used in previous builds of the *Thief* engine, which allowed for a great deal of power and flexibility on the part of the sound designers. Eric Brosius, the audio director on *Thief: Deadly Shadows,* flew down from Boston (Irrational Games was kind enough to let us hire him temporarily since he had worked successfully on two previous *Thief* titles) to Austin, Texas, where Ion Storm was located, to discuss his ideal features. When those were added to the Ion Storm audio team's preferences, the result was an excellent graphical user interface for the team to use.

While the functionality of the *DE:IW* engine was modeled after that of the *Thief* engine, *DE:IW*'s code was based on the *Unreal* engine, originally developed by Epic Games. Having used the *Unreal* engine from the time it was built, I think a comparison of its features with those of *DE:IW* is necessary to show the significant expansion of audio capabilities. *Unreal* was released in 1998 but had been in development at least three years before that. Therefore, I'm basing the established feature sets on the years 1996 and 2002, respectively, when the feature sets were in full use.

Unreal (PC, 1996):

▶ Up to 64 sounds played back at once

▶ Limit of 1 MB of sample data for songs through a maximum of 16 channels

▶ Sounds can be looping or one-shot

▶ Dolby Pro Logic surround sound

▶ Each actor (object) can have an ambient sound with a controllable radius

▶ Doppler shifting

▶ Zone-based six-tap reverb filter

▶ One channel of music at a time, controllable dynamically via a SpecialEvent tag

▶ Windows Multimedia and DirectSound driver implementation, 64 volume steps on non-MMX Pentiums, 128+ on MMX Pentiums

As you can see, *Unreal* was released during a transitional period in PC gaming technology: Windows 95 was not long out of the gate, and its sound capabilities were far from stable. Only in the last five years have hardware and OS developers been seeing gaming as a truly lucrative development investment.

Deus Ex: Invisible War (Xbox, PC, 2002):

▶ Up to 128 sounds played back at once

▶ Streamed music and ambience, up to three stereo streams at once

▶ Sounds can be looping or one-shot

▶ Sounds controllable via a "schema" system, which allows multiple sounds to play for any event or object with configurable randomization

▶ Dolby Digital surround sound

▶ Zone- and trigger-assignable music and sound

▶ Trigger-assignable music and sound

▶ Inner and outer radius for each sound

▶ Controllable distance-attenuation curve

- ▶ Physics texture–based sound database (to work with physics implementation)

- ▶ Reverb achieved through "wet" sound files, which have effects like reverb in them (a "dry" sound file contains only the sound and no effects)

The differences here are considerable. Each sound in *DE:IW* can be panned discretely to one of five speakers surrounding the player. Sounds are no longer individual files but objects with customized properties. *DE:IW* also was one of the first games to use a physics system; objects can bounce, slide, roll, and scrape much the way they would in reality, and they sound just as realistic.

Working with Programmers

The *DE:IW* programmers were all focused on a single vision presented by Harvey Smith, the project director, and Chris Carollo, the lead programmer. Essentially, our technology was to at least match that of *Thief 1* and *Thief 2*. That was an excellent mandate, but within it there was much room for divergent development practices; and with the complexity of *DE:IW*, it's a testament to the tenacity and hard work of the team that the sound managed to come out clean and even impressive. Here are some lessons learned from programmer interaction that went less than smoothly.

Lesson 1: Logical playback and good sound quality don't always go together.
Midway through the project, a programmer assigned to integrate weapon sound effects into the game approached me regarding what he planned to do with an automatic weapon. He was going to play a single sound repeatedly based on the weapon's refire rate, which changed depending on how much damage each shot incurred and other gameplay considerations.

This seemed like a great idea initially, but we soon discovered that the repetition of the single sound was incredibly irritating. Logically, the effect of a gun firing multiple times should be achieved by repeating the same sound, but actually eliciting the effect is more complex than the sum of its parts. I would have preferred to use a looped sound myself, but I lacked rock-solid proof that it would be better than a bunch of one-shot sounds (sounds that do not loop). Prototyping would have solved the problem, but it was also a good lesson for the programmer to file away.

Lesson 2: All the systems in a game, including audio, need to be properly integrated with each other. Understanding the dependency of one system on another is crucial. An example follows:

In *DE:IW*, the code for the player sounds was separate from the code for sounds in the player's world—the gameplay environment such as a level, also known as a map. This proved a good idea for a variety of reasons: (1) The player sounds could be in stereo—a small triumph—and the other sounds could be 3D-positional mono (a sound effect is one channel instead of two, but panned by the audio engine to different speakers based on its location relative to the player); (2) if necessary, the player's weapons could use entirely different sounds than would the weapons of a nonplayer character (NPC); and, most important, (3) the NPC code could recognize and parse player sounds independently, a separation that allowed NPCs' behavior to be affected by player weapon sounds alone so that if a player fired, the NPC could respond by attacking the player. (If another NPC fired a weapon, the NPC would not attack the NPC who fired.)

Even given this differentiation between NPCs and player sounds , the player sound set itself had a number of limitations that affected the game. One of the players' special abilities was to be able to control robots and, when doing so, to view the world from the robot's optical sensors. When this happened, player code was used; however, several robots used looping sounds for movement, and player code didn't support looped playback. All the player did was use one-shot footstep sound effects. Because the functionality for robot control was introduced close to the game's beta version release date, when the sound programmer was busy with more important tasks, very simple looping code that didn't support preloop and postloop sound playback was used for robot control. What resulted was a loop that stopped and started very abruptly. In the real world, when you switch on a treadmill, for example, you can hear it gradually ramp up to its set speed. When you switch it off, it ramps down. But for the various robots that moved around using treads, the code that was used activated a loop sound that began immediately at full volume, which sounded very unrealistic. This was a quality hit that no one had planned for, but it could have been prevented with foresight and advance planning.

Lesson 3: Assign tasks properly.

As mentioned earlier, programmer assignments shifted more than once during the course of the project. Where the producers and programmer leads fell short was in their failure to inform the audio staff of the changes. Likewise, the audio director fell short by not staying informed of the changes.

Midway through the project, the audio director wrote a list of what programmer was responsible for each game system so that the audio staff would know whom to talk to when it came to integrating audio into the game. Unfortunately, the list came too late in the process to avoid certain pitfalls during development, such as clarifying the priority of tasks and their related duties. Also the assignments changed several times, so the initial list was rendered useless within six months.

Lesson 4: Stick to a schedule.

The programmers' schedules were unorganized and incomplete until very late in the project. The schedules also lacked information about sound implementation and estimates on how long a task would take. As a result, audio integration happened on the fly, and it was often difficult for the audio team to get any bugs fixed because the programmer would be assigned to another task by the time the bugs were discovered.

Here's an example: At one point about halfway through the project, the audio team went through a build of the game and found that certain robots were missing sounds. Since several programmers handled robot behavior and integration, the audio team wasn't sure which programmer to talk to about integrating the sounds. It fell to the audio team to ask the lead programmer, who would connect them with the appropriate person, but that person wasn't always sure when they would have time to integrate the sounds. Estimates of "soon" and "later" were used more often than days, weeks, or months.

Solution

Giving the sound team responsibility for more integration of audio assets is an excellent answer to all these issues. Why rely on people who are unfamiliar with how something should function from a sound perspective when the audio team can integrate things faster and more effectively than programmers? Listing specifications for every object in the game that needs sound is another good way around the problems (**Figure 5.2**).

The Sentinoid spec list

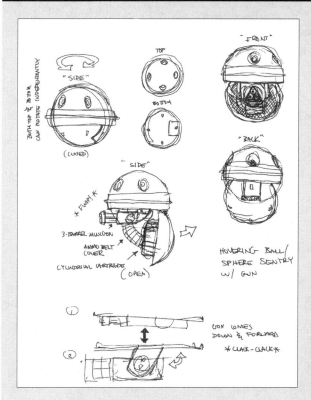

FIGURE 5.2 A spec list for a fictitious game's "floating sentinoid" character might look like this.

Name: Floating sentinoid.

Movement type: Looped engine sound with preloop and postloop start and stop.

Attack type: Laser, single shot, approximately .2 second in duration. Laser should be similar to the laser sound in *The Black Hole* but have plenty of varied versions of the same sound.

Additional behaviors: The sentinoid can sound an alarm once it sees the player. The alarm sound should loop or be a repeatable one-shot sound.

Comments: The sentinoid should sound as menacing as it looks. It is precise and very deadly.

Tech Limitations and Workarounds

Every game has its limitations, but *DE:IW* had far fewer of them than I had experienced when developing *Unreal*. There was more room to create different and more complex sounds for music as well as SFX; the sound quality was 16 bits across the board; it was much easier to integrate sounds into the player's world; and the game could play back a fairly large number of sounds. (By the way, 8-bit sound, which sounds horrible compared with 16 bits, was used regularly on major titles until as recently as five years ago.)

Until recently, when customized synthesis in game audio was replaced with the playback of recorded sound, technology severely limited audio development. Game audio began with recorded sound that was nearly unrecognizable and has progressed to the point where game audio is now threatening to overtake film audio in terms of its dramatic and immersive capabilities.

Despite such advances, *DE:IW* still had some technological limitations. For starters, real-time reverb was cut toward the end of the project. Originally each area of the game had its own reverb settings and the code added the right reverb to the sounds at each area (zone). Because processor capacity was close to the maximum and the additional work to assign and then debug and edit reverb zones would have proven too costly, the cut had to be made, to everyone's regret. However, the workaround was adding reverb to the sounds themselves in some places. A large, creaking wooden cathedral door benefited greatly from this and gave a much fuller sense of atmosphere in the level it was in.

Another limitation we encountered in *DE:IW* was the number of simultaneous streamed channels. We initially planned to cross-fade two stereo streams to achieve smooth music transitions and simple layering. In terms of code, this meant that at any given point a stereo stream would need to jump from playing two to four channels at once. Unfortunately, sound effects needed their own set of channels, and because cross-fading between streams (consisting of two channels each) was more important than playing more than one music track at the same time, we decided to keep one music track playing at a time and reserve a track for ambient sound streams. We worked around this limitation by providing one-shot music files that would play at key dramatic points in the game (sometimes called *stingers*), such as when a vent cover blows off during a terrorist attack and kills a passing guard.

What is often not considered a limitation is the game design itself and the paradigms that guide sound and music toward potentially unnecessary boundaries. I'll discuss this in detail in the next section.

Design and Creativity Report

Game design—the rules that govern how a game will operate, if you will—has exploded more than any other aspect of game creation. What was once a single-page description of mechanics can now fill volumes. In the development of *DX: IW,* design was law—more important than graphics or sound. Where design became a separate concern was in the way each team member understood it. *DE: IW*'s designers were able to present a focused design, but they had to refine it over months of collaboration. The initial design was far too ambitious to finish within the project's life cycle, so a great deal was cut and revised. Regardless, the lesson I learned was that for an audio team to succeed, it must align itself with the design of the game and its principles as outlined by the lead designer and the design document.

Meeting the Needs of the Game Type

Before the audio staff does anything, it must understand the game's type, or genre. For example, will a game be action oriented or puzzle based? Although *DE:IW* ended up redefining genres, its premise and setting were simple to understand. *DE:IW* was set in a science fiction–like future on Earth; the characters were people, and the actions (sneaking, shooting, talking, exploring, and so on) were familiar. What made *DE:IW* different was this: Because the game was sci-fi oriented, the player could augment the character he controlled to increase his abilities remarkably, such as the ability to jump twice as high as normal.

Music

With the game's setting and story in place, it was easy to come up with some raw ideas for music but difficult to nail down just how to integrate the music with the gameplay. With an action game it's easy to form an aggressive soundtrack in one's imagination. For a stealth game it's easy to imagine more subtle and suspenseful music. *DE:IW* had stealth, action, and more, so rather than base the soundtrack on genre, I decided to base it on the game's environments. We considered changing the soundtrack's intensity based on gameplay, but this would have proven distracting from the immersion: If the player is focused in any way on music within a game that is already highly realistic, the player starts to wonder where the music is coming from. (Is a band playing it? Is the player character wearing headphones?) This was a good enough reason to justify approaching the soundtrack from a more subtle angle. Besides, every game seemed to be going that route. Basing the soundtrack on environments proved to be a good idea, because it provided a slight emotional enhancement without distracting the player from sounds that were important for gameplay feedback—but it definitely resulted in a less dramatic effect. I later realized that people play games to escape reality (and play simulations to engage in a different kind of reality), and lifting them out of reality requires a stronger tweaking of the emotions and senses. More on this later.

Sound

From the beginning of the *DE:IW* project, sound effects and ambience were important for the interaction of nonplayer characters (who could hear the player and respond) as well as for player immersion. It wasn't hard to establish an easy design ethic to work from.

The project director, Harvey Smith, requested that sound be present in some form at all times. A game like *DE:IW* needed a lot of sonic feedback, because sound was to be used as a design element to guide the player through the game. While continuous sound wasn't exactly realistic, it had been done in *Thief* with great success. There was never to be silence, unless it was for dramatic purpose or another specific reason. This proved tough to implement; while there are many things in reality that emit sound all the time, the game's environments provided few sounds that the player could immediately associate with. Therefore the audio team was given power it had never had before: the ability to request that objects be placed in levels and even that new objects be created in the game. For example, we would notice an area that was sonically dead, like a simple office, and request that a coffeepot be added there. The coffeepot would make a simmering sound the way real ones do, and the space became more interesting after the simple addition of the object. *DE:IW* is still the most sonically complete game environment I have ever encountered, thanks to the efforts of the design team, Harvey, and most of all Todd Simmons, the game's sound engineer.

Elevating the Emotional Experience

Earlier I mentioned that the music in *DE:IW* was effective but almost too subtle. I think the music was perfect for the game, but it could have benefited from additional special triggered motifs. In particular, there was a place where the player activates an immense teleportation device the size of several aircraft hangars. The sounds in this area are powerful, but adding a musical swell upon the activation of the device would have made the player's eyes widen a bit more. But that's my opinion, and if you asked 20 other people you'd most likely get 20 different answers. After all, music is a more abstract concept to quantify than any other game element. Let's explore it a bit more.

Music

The term *immersive simulation* was used liberally during *DE:IW*'s production. The player was to experience a simulation from a first-person perspective, and, aside from the futuristic setting and the player's superhuman abilities, the feeling of being in the real world was very important. When we applied this need for realism to sound, it raised new considerations for the style of music. The music ended up being very subtle, somewhere between the music of the previous *Deus Ex* and the *Thief* titles; the former had full-blown songs with themes, and the latter had glorified ambient tones that shifted in the background. The design mandate that everybody agreed on was that the music was not to influence or distract the player in any way. This made perfect sense in a world that was to be presented realistically. After all, when we cross the street in real life, we don't do so because a piece of music tells us to. However, as mentioned earlier, games are not to imitate reality perfectly; they are meant to remove the player from it to some degree.

It was during *DE:IW*'s quality assurance and beta phase that I realized how profoundly a large segment of players rely on music. Feedback confirmed that many players were disappointed that the music took what they called "a backseat to the rest of the game." Designwise, I disagreed and still do, because the music served as a foundation for the entire experience. Some people expect music to have a lot of impact, and it was those people who thought the music was neglected. However, I do think the music could have enhanced an already dramatic situation more powerfully than it did.

Many games, specifically those with a 3D first-person perspective, have failed at creating a good atmosphere using an adaptive soundtrack, and I felt the original *Deus Ex* did too, even if it improved upon earlier methods. Unfortunately, we discovered during *DE:IW* that music didn't work the same way as the rest of the game when it came to systems. Each system was designed to let the player make a choice and react accordingly, in expected or unexpected ways. Music was most effective when it followed the moments in the game where the drama was scripted, and this could have been exploited far more than it was. In the future, this "scripting" of music in conjunction with dramatically scripted moments could also potentially be developed into code that could trigger emotional themes and motifs to play at appropriate points.

In any event, the takeaway was that I needed to play the game and design my music with greater attention to how the player felt at any given moment, and introduce more dramatic elements.

Voice Acting

Another example of the collision between design logic and dramatic presentation was the voice acting. Our system played back lines of dialogue without regard for timing between lines. We team members had grown used to the unrealistic nature of game conversations, but people who had never played the game observed that the conversations sounded robotic and were so unrealistic that they compromised the game's overall immersive effectiveness. The story itself was hailed as brilliant, but its dialogue and characterization could have been more believable. This problem is endemic in our industry.

Small Ideas, Big Returns

What follows is a list of audio development tips—suggested by me, Todd Simmons, and Eric Brosius—that improved the game tremendously. They were simple concepts, but when implemented they had a big effect on a wide range of areas.

Sound team control

While the idea of letting the sound team control the physics and implement the ambient sound seemed simple enough, it wasn't so easy to picture in terms of workflow. File management was controlled through Visual SourceSafe; if a sound designer had a map checked out, a level designer couldn't edit it. Initially and understandably, the producers were not convinced the idea was worth the risk of having designers relinquish control of all the maps they were responsible for building. Then a producer suggested that each sound designer could have control of one map for one day to make the necessary implementations of ambient sounds. Finally, a system was agreed on: Each level designer would be in charge of editing more than one map. Because each designer was unable to edit more than one map at a time, the sound team was free to edit any of the other maps while one was being worked on. With good communication, this system worked very well.

The result was astounding. There was a generational leap from *Deus Ex* to *DE: IW* because the interface improved drastically and the amount of time spent on making sure each map was thick with sound increased significantly. Because the level designers didn't have to do any sound work, they had more time to work on levels. And the sound team could use the time to integrate the sounds themselves instead of fixing problems generated by level designers, and thus got greater satisfaction from the entire team.

For the physics engine, the technology was brand-new and the workflow proved cumbersome. However, audio diagnostics that enabled the team to analyze objects that made the wrong sounds (or didn't make sounds at all) made debugging and tweaking easy.

DE:IW had a lot of objects that behaved according to relatively conventional laws of physics. Having them sound realistic was a difficult task but one that, as Warren put it, yielded a "stupidly powerful" system. Players heard things that they were so accustomed to that they hardly noticed them.

Nonstandard randomization

DE:IW didn't pioneer nonstandard randomization, but this was the first time I had seen it used, and I felt horribly idiotic for not having used it before. Chris Carollo mentioned that the game would use a randomization of sound playback with a bias against recently played (but not duplicated) sounds. This means that if seven footstep sounds are triggered when the player is walking, a different sound is played each time; each sound is different from the one that was played one or even two instances before. The sound code in the game engine looks in the entire set for sounds that have not yet been played and goes through all the existing sounds once before repeating a sound. This approach yields far less repetition than does simple randomization, which at times will play a sound twice in a row. The nonstandard randomization of so many sets of sounds (footsteps, gunshots, water droplets) boosted the overall sound quality.

When you open doors, you'll often discover others that connect with one another as well as those that lead in completely unexpected directions. Such was the nature of development on *DE:IW.* The plan was more ambitious than that of any other game I had heard of, and it ballooned into a development cycle filled with new and unexpected challenges, especially for audio. Regardless of the hardships, the team pulled together and made a game more than worthy of its predecessor's groundbreaking qualities.

CHAPTER 6
Ideal Workflow

WORKFLOW is a subject that's difficult to read about without falling asleep. To avoid this effect as much as possible, let's take a look at the big picture. I consider it my "under pain of death" responsibility to give industry veterans and newcomers alike a good sketch using broad strokes before delving into technical details. The first point to remember is that game industry veterans are still babies compared with veterans of other industries, and a lot of the mistakes being made by the "old hands" are the ones folks in other industries made ages ago.

In terms of process or workflow, the electronic game industry has evolved in much the same way that many other industries have, and it can be most closely associated with other aesthetic entertainment industries such as film and television. Strictly defined, as explained in Chapter 2, workflow is the way actions are combined over a period of time to achieve a desired result.

When the game industry was started, a few people came up with a completely new method of expression, creating images and sounds that engaged the player. Those who wrote code to create music loved doing it: Although the process was laborious, they got compositional feedback without needing to know how to play an instrument. I had this experience myself, being able to create virtuosity on a Chameleon Seequa PC (**Figure 6.1**) rather than rely on physical skill with a piano. This new method of development helped with every aspect of a game's creation, from graphics to sound. (Artists did not have to be skilled in traditional methods to create visually satisfying images.)

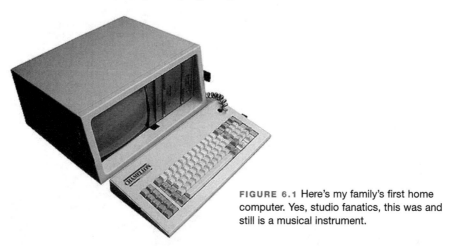

FIGURE 6.1 Here's my family's first home computer. Yes, studio fanatics, this was and still is a musical instrument.

Back then, game-audio developers didn't need a Foley studio and thousands of dollars' worth of gear to create something with the desired effect and proper feedback, because the medium they used—videogames—was based on the computer system with which they developed the audio. If you wanted a piece of music or a sound effect, you would simply sit down at a computer, write a few lines of code, and be done. Granted, sound effects and music weren't as impressive as what you heard in film or on television, but that didn't matter. This new medium was interactive, and that set it apart. It was the ultimate means of simplified creative expression. With this method came the capability for just one person to create entertainment, and the process to create it was easy enough that a piece of entertainment could be created in a single day—in some cases, in a single hour. In cases like this, people don't really think about process too much, especially if they don't have goals such as profit, innovation, or worldwide competition. Geeks with the passion for programming a bouncing ball usually just do it, regardless of whether they're doing it efficiently.

There was a period where games could be created to generate massive profit for very little work, and several developers (each represented by just one person or a handful of people) reaped huge benefits from this. The richest man I've ever met (he lives in a mansion complete with its own dungeon and observatory, owns sports cars, and plans to build a full-scale castle) is one of these pioneers. At present, however, companies must have process and workflow savvy or they don't succeed. In this chapter I'll explore techniques an audio team or individual can use to compete in today's fast-paced development environment.

Integrated Systems

It's not just for nostalgic purposes that I hark back to game development's olden days, although I do find a keen satisfaction in being able to say "Back in my day" to younger, bright-eyed aspiring audio folk. We're still in a transitional period in which some people still don't think or don't know that managing a game team is the single most difficult challenge in creating the game itself. The key point to remember is that audio isn't the only link in the chain to consider. A truly valuable member of the audio team, whether freelance or in-house staff, will be in tune (forgive the pun) with every other aspect of the project, even if only peripherally. You will be surprised by just how much something seemingly unrelated to audio can have a profound effect on it.

Dynamic Teams

As I've mentioned earlier, a game project is highly dynamic. You can establish the best-laid plans only to see them shift drastically mere months before shipping. The two biggest reasons for this are game design changes and technology changes. Whatever the reason, always bear in mind the dynamic nature of game development. Here are two primary examples of what can cause changes in project plans.

Focus group test results

Since the overall complexity of most games is increasing at a frightening rate, marketing departments often employ focus groups to find out whether the ideas of the design team lead or project director are good ones. A select group of people plays the game, and the results of many different tests are compiled; then, if the marketing department knows what it's doing, it can determine whether the game will sell a certain number of units. The process is very precise and, when done properly, very effective. In dramatic cases, focus group tests can reveal that large-scale changes in the game are necessary. This can cause panic and a great deal of rushing about on the part of the development team. A focus group needs to test a game as near to its shipping date as possible in order to get an accurate set of reactions and satisfaction ratings, but a game can be canceled altogether if a focus group determines it's a dud during testing.

This usually isn't nearly as nightmarish a situation for the audio staff as it is for the design team, programming staff, and artists. Bad audio can certainly ruin a game experience, but unless a game is utterly ear-shattering, it can ship and still be virtually as successful as it might have been with better music, sound effects, or voice acting.

Platform switcheroo, aka electric boogaloo

Another great threat to good workflow is the changing of a game's target hardware platform. This could happen if you were developing for the PC, for example, and the publisher or developer demanded that the game be written for the Sony PlayStation 2. Changing the platform means changing code, which adds even more time to the schedule than adding content such as art or audio does. A team of composers can write 20 minutes of excellent-quality music in a few days, but rewriting code to accommodate a new platform is much more complex. The process of changing the code is called *porting*, and programmers who are proficient at it are in very high demand.

Just to give you an idea of the amount of time it takes to port a title, it took well over a year to port *Deus Ex* from the PC to the PlayStation 2. Initially it was expected to take only six months; however, the resources of the new target platform were more limited than those of the original platform, and the schedule ended up ballooning to about a year. On a PC you can have a lot more available RAM and hard disk space. On a console such as the PlayStation 2, RAM is limited to 2 MB for audio. More can be used, as the system has 32 MB total, but for most titles 2 MB has become standard. Furthermore there's no hard disk, only what is called *streaming* from DVD, the format that the PlayStation 2 uses to store all game data. While streaming has reached great levels of capability, it still doesn't come close to the hard drive in its ability to process a lot of data (that is, more tracks of music and sound effects) in a short amount of time.

Switching platforms also has an impact on the audio team members, who often have to trim individual file sizes and also perhaps the number of files for music, voice, and sound effects to make the same amount of audio fit in the space allocated to the target platform for porting.

Focus groups and platform switches alone are perhaps the most drastic examples of what can change the game development process, but they're only two among many. In the next section I will examine how to manage information systems to be prepared for developmental changes.

Understanding the Management of Information Systems

Understanding a systems approach requires a bit of explanation, so let me take a moment to relate my understanding of it.

My father works in the corporate world as a business consultant. He has steered many top companies (Kraft Foods, IBM, Empire) toward running their business the right way, and I don't remember a case where he led anyone astray. Until I was about 12, I had no idea what my dad's work was. One day while passing a bookshelf as a young boy, I saw a couple of three-ring binders printed with the words *Information Continuum* and an infinity symbol with arrows along it. It was absolutely fascinating and absolutely perplexing. I eventually came to realize that my dad worked with computers (hence the word *Information* on the binder) and wanted to use computers to help people do business more efficiently for greater profit and greater customer satisfaction. However, his knowledge encompassed more than computer-related business models. Likewise, his understanding of the term *systems* wasn't applied just to computers, but also to a variety of business processes (hence the word *Continuum*, meaning *range*).

To a kid, this stuff is boring. It's boring to many adults too, especially musicians. Little did I know that systems applied to my life even at age 12: A system is vital in order for any group (of any size or any age) to work with any other group and have anything good come out of it. Besides charisma and good communication, knowing how things work together in any project involving more than one person—on a theoretical as well as a practical level—is necessary to make things work well for any member of a team, but especially for management.

Now I'll explain how systems and the ownership of systems apply to audio, and then I'll explore how they apply to other disciplines.

Audio ownership: titles

A lot of terms get thrown around among audio folk, from *mastermind* to *monkey*. In the game development world, people describe someone's job and responsibilities using whatever terms they want. In this section, I'm using the game-audio professional titles generally accepted by a large portion of the industry. In fact, I will treat this section like the audio "monster manual" of game development.

As you may recall, in Chapter 2 ("Workflow") I talked about the audio titles you should avoid using. Here are the titles you should use and what they mean.

Audio director: This person usually runs one or more audio departments at a large development or publishing company. The audio director usually doesn't provide content but instead focuses on managing departments. Responsibilities include maintaining budgets and schedules; ensuring that the audio team is properly trained to integrate audio as well as produce it where necessary; overseeing game audio from a general perspective; and dealing with the odd administrative task such as requesting equipment, outsourcing, and licensing content owned by other companies or organizations.

Audio manager: The audio manager has responsibilities similar to those of a director but is usually in charge of only one project at a time (like an audio lead) and is responsible for fewer staff members.

Audio lead: The audio lead is the point person for an individual project. Unlike a director or a manager, however, the audio lead is usually not responsible for budgets or administrative duties beyond scheduling. The audio lead has the ultimate understanding of a project's content needs and can direct the audio staff to create that content.

Lead composer: A lead composer is simply the best composer on a team, with skills that may even surpass those of the audio lead or audio director. The audio lead can point to the lead composer as an example for the other composers. Sometimes a lead composer doubles as an audio lead.

Composer: A member of the audio staff who writes music.

Lead sound designer: The best sound designer on a team. The lead sound designer can double as the audio lead, though less often than a lead composer doubles as the audio lead.

Sound designer: This person creates the sound effects.

Sound engineer: A sound engineer is trained to use the proper equipment for recording sessions (such as mixing boards, compressors, microphones, and amplifiers) and those tasks performed by the composer and sound designer. When the composer and sound designer are focusing on creating content, a sound engineer's equipment expertise can be invaluable. A sound engineer may also have knowledge of mixing and mastering. With such knowledge, a sound engineer can function as a type of integration engineer, defined below.

Integration engineer: This member of the audio staff is trained to integrate music and sound effects into the game engine itself. The integration engineer knows how to incorporate content created by composers and sound designers and make it work properly in the game.

Now that I've defined a robust and effective audio department, I'll move on to define the ownership of programming systems.

Nonaudio ownership: systems

Ownership of systems can be explained simply in terms of who does what. Here's an example description of a system and its ownership:

System: Weapons code

System description: Code that defines weapon behavior including design specification (spec), animation control, particle effects, and audio hookup

Owner: John Broomhall

If you still remember the development process map (DPM) at this point, bless you. Such a document can (and should) be used for code systems but seldom is. However, in this case let's say that there is a code DPM and it defines various segments of code as they relate to the game. *Make sure this code DPM includes an audio specification.* All too often a programmer comes to the audio team with no idea of what the object they're responsible for will sound like or how it will behave soundwise. The audio team can solve this problem by defining the spec well in advance; additionally, such a spec should be copied to the sound-design document (see Chapter 1, in the section "Establishing Functionality"). Now that we have taken care of the *what* in *who does what,* let's tackle the *who.*

Steady Communication

Communication—that is, actually talking to the people you work with— is crucial. Whether you're just breaking into freelance game audio, you're starting a job with a major developer or publisher, or you've been developing game audio for years, it's easy to forget some basic lessons of communication. As a result, game development companies the world over are starting to employ management and administrative techniques that have already been developed by the world's leading nongame companies. These techniques have been evolving over the last hundred years, but that doesn't mean that old-fashioned, basic lessons of communication get shoved behind the latest organizational development master classes.

Communication is just as important a skill for the audio staff as it is for the rest of the game team. Unfortunately, communication breakdowns happen all the time. They exist in many forms.

Examples of Communication Breakdowns

Problem	Solution
Someone holds a meeting and is unsure who will need to provide input at the meeting. As a result, some people get left out.	Consult with the producer, or whoever manages task assignments, about who would benefit from and contribute to a meeting.
People go to a meeting but later forget what was resolved.	Someone at the meeting takes notes on the decisions made, then distributes the report to everybody who attended.
Someone feels nervous about discussing a sensitive issue, such as speaking critically to someone in a senior position about a problem they have with a decision that the person made.	This employee needs to approach the issue as honestly and respectfully as possible. While this individual might not need to speak quite so tactfully with a peer on the team, bringing up an issue with a more senior person requires greater discretion. The nervous emotion should not prevent the employee from raising the issue, especially if the issue is of high importance.
Someone forgets one of the company procedures.	A peer or supervisor reminds the person of the procedure. If the person forgets more than three times, some kind of disciplinary action is taken.

These are only four examples of fairly standard communication issues, but they still happen all the time. In addition to the lessons learned with our meeting examples in Chapter 1, "A Development Process Map (DPM) of Game-Audio Implementation," if you begin with these as a foundation for learning to communicate properly in your next project, you may find yourself one step ahead of the people who hired you.

Solid Schedules

In Chapter 1 we discussed how to define technology, implementation (workflow), design, and asset preparation. We learned how to create a DPM so that by the end of preproduction, all planning for the work that needed to be done for production was finished. Once that planning is finished, however, the audio director or manager needs to create a schedule from that DPM.

A schedule is your blueprint. It's where you look to build that thing that you call your work—what you do on a game. Sounds so simple it's almost insulting, doesn't it? You might be surprised that there are still a lot of game companies that don't know how to schedule properly, because scheduling is like Othello, chess, and playing the guitar: very easy to learn, and very difficult to master. Microsoft Project is a fine tool for displaying your schedule (**Figure 6.2**).

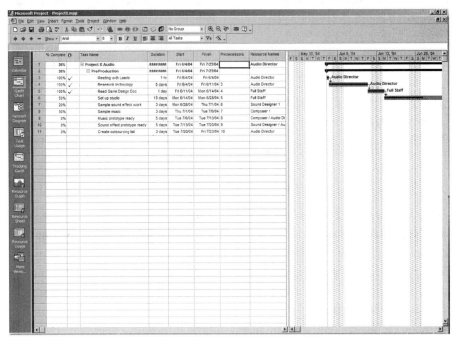

FIGURE 6.2 Microsoft Project is an excellent way to display a schedule, but it is by no means a replacement for a development process map (DPM).

The game-audio industry, as well as many other industries, uses the term *crunch time*. Some of us know this term all too well and have heard tales of employees sleeping at work for months on end, barely able to see their families for more than a couple of hours each day during periods of intense production. These horror stories have caused the start of a rebellion against crunch time, and proper scheduling is one of the ways to beat it.

In this section I'll review some techniques to guide audio production to fruition with a minimum of crunch time.

Be Ready at the End of Preproduction

Once we had a DPM, we were able to use it to create our asset list, so essentially we're prepared to build a schedule. However, schedules change and so do DPMs. One thing affects another, and keeping track of all the changes becomes more difficult as dependencies increase.

If the DPM and asset list follow the game design document by the time production begins, that's as much as anyone can do to stay up-to-date. Just remember to keep checking the game design document for any changes (also known as "feature creep"), and if the document hasn't changed in months, ask for updates from the lead designer or project director. Keep in mind that it's easy to neglect the updating of documentation during crunch time, so make sure your documentation as well as the design team's is up-to-date. Before preproduction ends, quite a few changes are usually made to the game design document, because preproduction is the stage where design is related to code.

How long it takes to code all the features determines whether all of the game design team's wishes can be met. Designing a project successfully means it will be able to meet its schedule and budget. The timeline for an average major title is 18 to 24 months; the game design should take into account whether a predetermined number of programmers can code the game's required functionality within that time. To manage costs, the publisher often puts a "lock" on the programming team and schedule—meaning they are unchangeable. When such a lock is not put in place, a development team that's not already proven may spend millions of dollars beyond an initial budget, potentially causing serious damage to the publisher.

This "shaving" of game design is also known as a reality check. Be ready to rearrange quite a few things in your asset list and DPM if and when this process takes place, and make sure the lead designer makes you aware of changes to the design document so you can make these rearrangements. Once production begins, prepare for more reality checks. Throughout this process, staying on top of design and code by identifying areas that will affect audio (such as code changes to a particle system that triggers sounds when particles appear), as outlined in the DPM, will make life much easier when future changes are made.

Technology Lock

Because games are creative and aesthetic products, the technology must serve the design as much as it can. Unfortunately, as I've demonstrated with the reality check process, code can achieve only so much to provide design with the functionality required, so locking technology is an excellent way to keep design in check.

By locking technology, I mean finalizing a system—such as adaptive music or sound effects randomization—as early on as possible and changing nothing about it aside from fixing bugs that keep it from functioning.

The exception (which can sometimes be built into the code schedule) is to reserve some coding time in the schedule so that a programmer can create a feature or tool for the audio staff that will speed up production or put it back on schedule.

Because musicians and sound designers often deal with extremely puzzling and limiting technology to reproduce sound in games, an audio team is often expected to be able to create great things from limited resources. Therefore, locking technology is a contingency audio teams should be prepared to deal with.

Intelligent Estimating

Estimating task time is a basic requirement of creating the DPM and the sound-design document, but it is one of the most difficult and critical tasks involved in creating a schedule. Suppose a composer has no idea how long it will take to write a particular piece of music, or—even more difficult to determine—how long it will take to integrate that music.

To estimate task times intelligently, you need to take data from previous projects and use it wisely, not hastily. When estimating tasks, the person doing the production (a sound designer or composer) should give the estimates to an audio director, who will take the estimates and schedule them properly. Also time yourself and others on tasks or groups of tasks, and record the results, preferably in the asset spreadsheet. These results eventually will be valuable for work in an existing or future project. Since larger tasks—such as the creation of all object sounds for a game—are rarely completed from start to finish in a single work session, it's also very important to record what interrupts work on the task and what holds back the work.

Keep the following points in mind when recording task completion time:

▶ Specify whether the task was completed in a single session. Sometimes sound designers and composers work on multiple files simultaneously.

▶ Specify whether the task was completed with all its required tools ready, or if tools had to be created to complete the task. For example, the sound designer or composer might need a plug-in before they finish an asset to satisfaction. Making such a specification will require a record of the time it takes to complete the task and create the necessary tools.

▶ Voice recording for dialogue can be tricky to estimate, as it includes the time it takes not only for the actor to record the line correctly with guidance from a voice director, but also for the audio director or lead designer to choose a line from among multiple takes. It's best to tally the amount of time to record a certain number of lines devoted to a particular segment of the game (such as a level).

▶ For the purposes of integrating audio into the game, again try to make estimates in discrete segments. For example, how long did it take to integrate all the character animation sound effects for the running back Chris Carter in the latest NFL title? How long did it take to integrate all the one-shot music motifs played in the dungeon level in the latest role-playing game?

These estimates all go in your DPM and sound-design document and are used by the audio director to create an initial schedule.

Task lists

Here are several common lists of tasks; you can use these as a general-purpose guide for any game genre.

Production These tasks are for the assets themselves.

Music:

▶ Ambient (music that plays in the background)

▶ Layered (music that layers on top of the ambient music)

▶ One-shot or scripted (music that plays for a particular event)

▶ FMV (full-motion video; usually applies to nongameplay parts of the game the player watches, such as movies and cut scenes)

Sound effects:

▶ HUD/UI (heads-up display/user interface; applies to things that the player uses that are not in the game world but superimposed on it in some fashion, such as the text that lists the score, or an inventory)

▶ Character (applies to player characters and nonplayer characters, or NPCs)

▶ Ambient (sounds that play in the background, providing ambience)

▶ Object (sounds specific to objects)

▶ FMV (full-motion video; same as with music)

Voice:

▶ Barks (the lines that play when the player encounters an NPC but do not lead to a conversation, such as comments like "Hello"; also known as *broadcast speech*)

▶ Conversation (the lines that follow after the player initiates a dialogue with an NPC)

▶ FMV (full-motion video; same as with music and sound effects)

Integration   Integration differs greatly from asset production, though the list may be the same. Each of the following applies to whatever systems and tools the programmers on the team will provide to the audio staff. For instance, HUD/UI sound effects integration may not have a tool to integrate them (it is still common for a programmer to do the job), but it is still the responsibility of the audio director or manager to track how long it takes to integrate those sound effects.

Music:	Sound effects:	Voice:
▶ Ambient	▶ HUD/UI	▶ Barks
▶ Layered	▶ Character	▶ Conversation
▶ One-shot or scripted	▶ Ambient	▶ FMV
▶ FMV	▶ Object	
	▶ FMV	

Backup Plans

The best laid plans… OK, we've heard that one before, haven't we? The title of this section is self-explanatory, but I'll add some detail to humor the people who plunked down their disposable dollars for this book.

I can't count the number of times I have told people, "I'd rather not do that, but if we have to, we can work with it." Here's an example. When I was working on *Unreal* six years ago—in ancient times, technologically speaking—I didn't want to use 8-bit sounds for sound effects or music. At any discernible low volume, the sounds had a crackly hiss. Unfortunately, at the start of the project, the programmer of the sound engine told me that support for 16-bit sounds would be too costly. Just a year or so later, however, it was fairly obvious that most games were using 16-bit sounds, even if they were 11 kHz (CD quality being 44 kHz).

By that time, more than half of the music in *Unreal* had been made with 8-bit sounds, but the musicians scrambled to upgrade their samples, and the sound effects guy upgraded quite a few of the sounds as well. Why weren't all the sounds switched to 16 bits? The reason was that they hadn't been saved as 16 bits, and 8-bit sounds cannot simply be converted to 16 bits for better sound quality. Once they're at 8 bits, that crackly hiss is there to stay. This is a perfect example of what not to do. The samples and sound effects should have been made at 16 bits from the beginning.

Therefore, at the start of the project, look ahead and try to plan as much as possible for change. Build this advance planning—also known as buffer time or "we f*#%ed up" time—into schedules as well. If at the beginning of a project, for example, you think that 24-bit sounds might be possible down the line, create your sound effects in 24 bits initially and down-sample them (convert them to 16 bits) when it's time to integrate sound into the game. And if 24-bit audio gets a green light in the meantime, you'll have those pristine 24-bit versions ready to go rather than create the sounds all over again.

Feature Lockdown and the Fuzzy Beta Definition

A game is typically worked on until the last minute, meaning that content and code are changed until the game is burned to a CD, given a rather complicated series of tests, and packaged to ship to stores. This happens even at Electronic Arts, which boasts a postproduction segment in its development cycle, and nowhere is it more difficult to finalize than in audio. In the production of most big-budget feature films, the film is done before audio is mixed and music scored. Not so with games. Let's see how we can handle this challenge and squeeze more out of postproduction. But first, I'll define terms that apply to the final stages of a project's schedule: *feature/content lockdown, alpha, beta, RC (release candidate),* and *gold*.

Finality for Audio

What makes an audio asset final? Is it final when it's produced? When it's integrated? When it's integrated and mixed? When the leads sign off on it? Yes, yes, yes, and yes.

Making the audio and integrating it into the game is the easy part when it comes to finalization, though, at least from the audio team's perspective. At this point—the end of production—audio and the way it is integrated are subject to comments from people who have no context for describing objections they might have. (For example, the comment "This gun sound sucks" doesn't help the audio team fix that sound in the context of the entire set of gun sounds; more information is required.) Anyone from the lead designer to the quality assurance (QA) testers can weigh in with their opinion.

The audio director should use discretion when it comes to changing sounds after they've been integrated. Changing an integrated sound could affect another part of the game adversely. For example, in response to the "This gun sound sucks" complaint, changing a treble-heavy gun sound so that it includes more low frequencies (a common request) may help the weapon sound more powerful, but it might also make the entire sound mix in a game level already filled with bass too overwhelming.

A good system for tracking the status of sounds is to have various phases of approval for a sound effect, from creation to integration to lockdown. There should be a point at which all the leads on the team consider a sound final, after which the sound can be changed only if a large number of bugs are reported by, say, more than five people on the team or in QA. Tracking these phases using check boxes or buttons in the sound asset spreadsheet is an effective practice.

Postproduction is where sounds and the mix are made final. If the QA staff is testing the game before the sound engineers have had a chance to mix the integrated sounds properly, be ready for comments like "This sound is too loud," "This sound needs more bass," and "I can't hear this sound." Make sure the entire team is aware of the status of the mix as well.

Using QA for Good Feedback

The QA testers are your friends: They are the folks who get copies of the game in various stages and test rigorously for bugs, report them in a database, then do more testing and more reporting until the game is considered complete. Below I describe the various stages at which a game is tested. Note that these definitions are fairly standard, but they may vary from publisher to publisher.

Feature/content lockdown: The game is considered complete in terms of features and content, meaning all the functionality and assets are in the game. The features may not all be functional and the assets may not yet be used correctly, but they're all in. This term is being used more and more in conjunction with *alpha,* but often *alpha* is used to describe only content.

Alpha: The content—artwork, animation, sound, music, and so on—is complete and integrated, but the code may not be even close to final. *Alpha* is a technical term for a goal that the entire game team shoots for, but at this stage the game is rarely complete, since content is often tweaked right until the game ships.

Beta: The content and code are complete, but the game isn't necessarily free of bugs. Beta differs from feature/content lockdown because all the code necessary to make the features work properly may not be present.

RC (release candidate): A "build," or version of the game, is burned to the format on which it will be shipped (DVD, cartridge, or CD). A build is considered bug free when it is sent to QA and the testers find no bugs that they deem important enough to fix. (Some bugs are cosmetic—for example, the look of a texture.)

Gold: The final version of the game. A *gold master*—a CD or DVD—is sent to a duplicator, which then creates a *glass master* (a CD or DVD that is used to create thousands, sometimes millions of copies) and pumps out products for shipping.

QA will send bug reports to the audio team, and the reports should be treated with respect. Doing so will give QA more reason to report bugs that you can agree on. As far as how QA treats the audio team, proceed to the next section.

Using a Bug Database and Prioritizing Fixes

The bug database is an ingenious creation. The audio team can benefit greatly from this database, as it can turn a "This song sucks" e-mail into valuable criticism. It is like any other database, with fields of information—in this case, data about bugs—that can be configured however the user likes, as well as information vital to fixing problems in the game. The QA team and the game team as a whole, including audio, use this database to move a game speedily from alpha to gold. Here's a rundown on good database field information. A report on a bug should include the following details.

Bug number, bug title, the date and time reported, and the name of the person reporting the bug: This clerical information is important for referencing the bug. Management may wish to set limits on who may create bug reports, but usually the producer or QA manager is the one who sifts through reports entered by the entire team and prioritizes them. Also keep in mind that a bug title should be descriptive but short.

Priority: Usually categorized by letter. An A bug is high priority and should be fixed before any B bug.

Bug assignment: This is one of the most difficult fields to get right. It's one thing to manage many bug reports submitted by different people on the team, but if a bug fix is assigned to the wrong person, quite a bit of time can be wasted. The solution is to allow only certain people the right to assign a bug fix in the first place. At Electronic Arts, a bug report is initially sent to the producer (aka the director of development, that almighty manager who knows and sees all), who then assigns the fix to the correct person. To save the director time, however, information can be put on an intranet site outlining who is in charge of a particular system. Remember that ownership bit we discussed earlier in the chapter? That can be invaluable here.

Bug description: This is another field that needs careful management. A good bug report does not contain comments like "This sucks" or "This is not good." It may contain the statement "I don't like this," but it will also state why, including a brief but thorough explanation. Here's an example of all the field entries discussed so far:

Bug #10293

Bug title: Sacred palace music cuts off

Priority: C

Date, time reported: 6/3/2004, 12:05 p.m.

Bug reported by: Kiana Reeves

Bug assigned to: Bill Bixby

Bug description: When entering the sacred palace, the music cuts off but the sound effects still play. I've checked to see if this happens on other test machines and it happens on every one, in the same circumstance. Is this supposed to happen?

Additional comments/replies: Whoever the bug fix is assigned to can respond in this field by asking for clarification. This person can also clarify whether the so-called bug is actually a "nonbug" or "not an important bug," or can recommend that the bug fix be assigned to someone else.

Make sure you and your team enter bug reports efficiently and effectively, under-standing the other issues plaguing the game so that you don't inundate folks with issues when they're already under the gun. Choose your battles.

One thing I've learned in dealing with QA is that educating the QA depart-ment about the game audio is invaluable. Letting them know the aesthetic of the audio, and its functionality, can prevent a lot of reports being made for "bugs" that are simply unfinished integration, are supposed to be there, and so forth.

The Audio Team's Responsibilities

Speaking of choosing your battles, this book is about getting the respect you deserve as an audio developer—but to achieve that, you need to deserve it in the first place. You can do that by taking to heart the following lessons, learned by yours truly from personal experience. Use them well.

▶ Realize you have finite time and a finite budget. You might have dreams of creating the best audio in the world, but unless you can fit it into the sched-ule and under budget, it won't happen. You and the producer need to see eye-to-eye.

▶ Keep your nonaudio leads informed and educated. The leads won't be walk-ing into the studio every few days, at least most of the time. They want you to be self-managing as much as possible. Make sure they know what your problems are. When you self-manage, you solve most of your own problems without their help anyway. More often than not, they will be happy to help you with the big ones.

▶ Make sure the nonaudio leads sign off on decisions. Do *not* go behind backs. I've done this without realizing it, and what happens isn't pretty. In some cases it might take beating down a door and screaming to make it clear that you're going to make a decision about something that everyone might not agree with but that you believe is in the title's best interests. If someone else has made a decision that you're not happy with, and your opinion gets overruled after you bring it up one more time, it's usually a good idea to let it drop. There are other battles to fight, and as I hope I've taught you (actu-ally, Sun Tzu, as well as others, taught me): Every battle is won before it's ever fought.

▶ Don't be a yes-person. It's easy to give in to pleasing people, but don't agree to everything. Try to come up with a backup plan for things you can't do. For example, you might not be able to have as many sounds as others would like because of space restrictions. As a backup plan, you could determine which sounds in the game are vital and which can be deleted. Organize them accordingly in your sound asset spreadsheet, and you'll know which ones can be cut first. If you aren't sure whether you can fulfill a request, investigate it before you agree to it. Above all, be honest about your limitations or disagreements, even if you think you'll get a scowl or two.

▶ Encourage the leads to make their decisions clear. As my friend and colleague Kurt Harland taught me, if a lead isn't clear—in fact, if *anyone* isn't clear— it's wonderful to be able to say, "I'm not sure what you're talking about." Saying this has never gotten me in trouble, and it helps tremendously in everyday conversation as well as in meetings and e-mails.

CHAPTER 7
Ideal Production

YOU CAN'T DISCUSS game audio without understanding how it's produced, so I am devoting this chapter to that process. I will attempt to describe the most effective ways to create the best game audio possible.

For starters, ideal production requires creating audio assets while keeping foremost in mind their integration into the game. Here's a simple but apt example: If you've created a sound effects file that is the sound of a footstep on concrete, you should group it with other footsteps on concrete. Ideal production leads to easier integration.

In the last five years alone, game-audio production has changed drastically. Not too long ago, only a select few could create game audio, let alone integrate it. Now, anyone who can wield an instrument or hold a microphone can see that music and sound for games are not so different from those for film—right until the integration begins, at which point the similarities between film and game audio end. Game audio is whatever you want it to be: If your influence is film, then your games can sound like films. While I happen to be influenced by films a great deal, I will use this chapter to show how you can generate your own unique flavor of audio.

I will also focus on areas that directly affect production, such as marketing considerations and legal issues.

The Fat Pipeline

One of the most important aspects of production is the proper linking of tasks with techniques to achieve the desired results. In this section I will discuss how to streamline your production chain to create high-quality assets—music, sound effects, and voice. In his excellent book *The Fat Man on Game Audio: Tasty Morsels of Sonic Goodness,* George Alistair Sanger describes his music-writing process in a good amount of detail, including information about the computers and software he uses. This is perhaps the best practical information in the book and is absolutely fascinating. Don't let the fact that I was its technical editor deter you from buying a copy.

George's book is the primary source for much of the solution I will present for music and sound effects production. To illustrate this process, I have created a version of the development process map and affectionately called it the Fat Pipeline (**Figure 7.1**).

Many books (such as *The New Recording Studio Handbook,* by John M. Woram and Alan P. Kefauver) go into greater detail about how to set up a studio for various means of production, so I will just briefly describe the options. Many of you may already know how to set up an audio studio, as thousands of people outside the game industry have already done this.

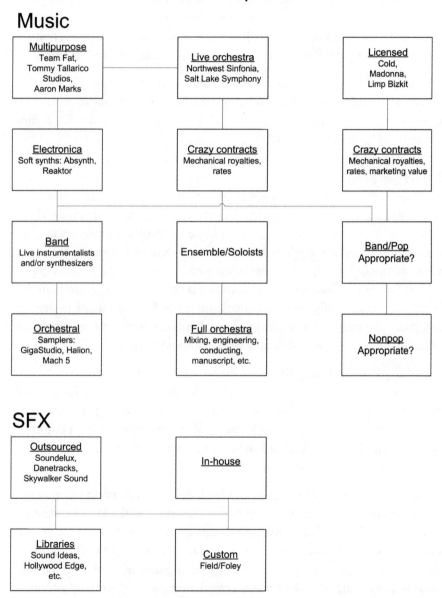

FIGURE 7.1 The Fat Pipeline. The most successful methods of creating music and sound effects are multipurpose production, using a live orchestra, and licensing. Related issues include technology, marketing, and contracts.

Music Production

Currently the three popular schools of music production are multipurpose production, a live orchestra, and licensing. The kicker is that the technology for all of these methods differs only a little bit. It's *how* the technology is linked that gives the composer either an advantage or a serious setback in production.

Note that I have made some assumptions for this pipeline; for example, I'm assuming all recording and editing is being done by a PC. Sometimes other equipment is used, but the versatile PC is rapidly replacing methods such as tape recording via Tascam DA-88 and ADAT.

Multipurpose production

Multipurpose production is, as its name denotes, the Swiss army knife of music production, and it constitutes roughly 75 percent of all game music today. There are more than 1000 multipurpose game-audio music production houses in existence. (Such "houses" are anything from a 10-by-10–foot bedroom to a luxurious, equipment-stocked studio.) Team Fat is one well-known example of this type of production house; Tommy Tallarico Studios is another among a vast pool of talent. Each house usually employs a small number of folks, from one to five individuals, who compose a variety of styles of music. I once ran a multipurpose production house as a freelancer; now I am employed by one.

In the olden days (from the 1980s until the late '90s), a multipurpose production house could create music on multiple platforms, but all the music consisted of the infamous bleeps and bloops we refer to when we think of game music in its early years. Now, a multipurpose house must create not only cross-platform music that can play on an Xbox, a PlayStation 2, and so on, but also multiple genres of music, from country to electronica.

Even in the early days of game-music production, it was well worth composers' time to learn multiple platforms—say, Nintendo, Sega, and the PC—because a company would be more likely to hire a composer or team who was able to create audio for all of these. Creating cross-platform music isn't the difficult part anymore. Now it's generally simpler to create cross-platform music because you can easily convert digital audio files between the various platforms. (However, today's highly adaptive scores use technically complex assets such as MIDI + sample banks, instead of digital audio files, thus making it harder to port the music from the original platform to another.) But the primary challenge is finding the appropriate musical style and genre. This will be a recurring theme as we explore the Fat Pipeline.

Electronica

Electronica—also known as *techno*—encompasses a genre of music that includes subgenres such as jungle, ambient, and house. Electronica is the type of music that's the quickest to generate, as one person can create it from start to finish without the use of live instrumentalists. For more information on this style, I highly suggest you visit the All Music Guide Web site (`www.allmusic.com`). It has good descriptions that let you know what you're talking about if you're a publisher looking for a composer to hire, or if you're a composer looking to score a gig.

The following setup is all you need to create electronica, and we will use the power of the DPM to display a further level of detail (see **Figure 7.2**).

As you can see, as far as equipment is concerned it's easy to start writing this genre of game music. But don't be fooled. Once you get started with the software, you'll see it's as if you'd walked into several rooms filled with knobs, sliders, and tiny text readouts. These rooms contain your software-based synthesizers—in this case, Native Instruments' Abysnth and Reaktor, both of which can create incredibly varied and complex sounds; they are among the top synthesizer programs on the market. My advice to those who want to create more original-sounding electronica: Experiment with your instrument or synthesizer of choice. At least 50 percent of your music is the instrumentation, and choosing that instrumentation may well take up 50 percent of your composition time. For more information, check out the article I wrote on the importance of instrumentation, at `www.gamasutra.com/features/20040430/brandon_01.shtml`. (Note: Gamasutra requires that you sign up in order to read the article. There's no charge to register.)

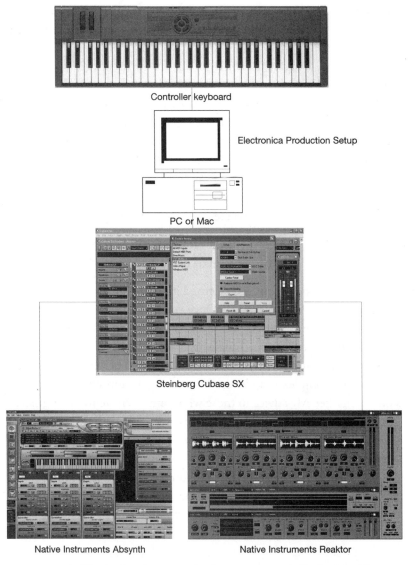

Controller keyboard

Electronica Production Setup

PC or Mac

Steinberg Cubase SX

Native Instruments Absynth   Native Instruments Reaktor

FIGURE 7.2 In this simple software synthesizer setup, a controller keyboard is connected to a PC via a MIDI interface. The PC is running Cubase SX as a multitrack editor for sequencing the input from the keyboard with the Native Instruments software synthesizers Absynth and Reaktor.

Bands

When electronica won't suffice, live instruments (or synthesizer-based approximations) are called for. We're all familiar with the typical band structure: a guitar, a bass, a drum kit, some form of a keyboard (either a piano or an organ, sometimes a custom synthesized instrument), and a vocalist (see **Figure 7.3**). Multipurpose composers can achieve the sound in a number of ways. Team Fat plays its own music, as it has four main members and can easily hire other local musicians. Tommy Tallarico records a few tracks himself and hires contract studio players for the rest, and sometimes even has studio players do the entire thing.

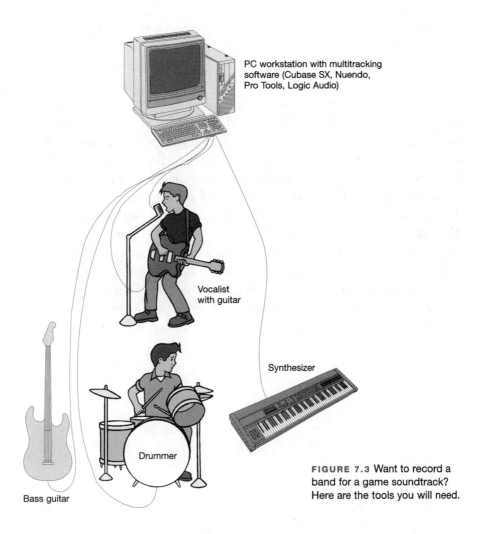

PC workstation with multitracking software (Cubase SX, Nuendo, Pro Tools, Logic Audio)

Vocalist with guitar

Synthesizer

Drummer

Bass guitar

FIGURE 7.3 Want to record a band for a game soundtrack? Here are the tools you will need.

Recording the instruments for a band calls for a setup a bit more complicated than for electronica, but it all depends on how many tracks you wish to record simultaneously. For example, a number of inputs to a mixer all must be monitored simultaneously if you record a guitarist, a bassist, and a drummer at the same time. You need to make sure their volume levels are set properly and sound good together (the drums shouldn't overpower the bass, and vice versa) before you begin recording. With electronica, recording is often done one track at a time; additional inputs are not required.

Orchestras

Orchestral music is perhaps the fastest-growing segment of the multipurpose composition pipeline. Individual instruments from violins to tubas, as well as groups of those instruments (first violins, second violins), are being recorded and turned into instrument "patches" (instruments you play using keyboard synthesizers) that can be controlled in the same way an electronica instrument can, with knobs and sliders to adjust sound aspects such as volume and pitch for filter parameters such as attack and decay. Top it off with all possible performance capabilities (portamento, staccato, spiccato) by the instruments, and you have nearly a dead ringer for a live performance. A flute staccato note and a tuba legato note can be linked so that they play at the same time when a single key on the controller keyboard is pressed. The same kind of sampling technique is being done for choirs. Take a look at the diagram for the setup (**Figure 7.4**). It's more complex than for electronica production, but less so than for a five-piece band in terms of outboard equipment. You will notice that because of the vast sizes of these recorded instruments, entire PCs are devoted to funneling them to the central PC on which the multipurpose composer multitracks. Popular multitracking software such as Cubase SX is needed to manage these vast samples and complex instruments.

PC workstation with multitracking
software (Cubase SX, etc.)

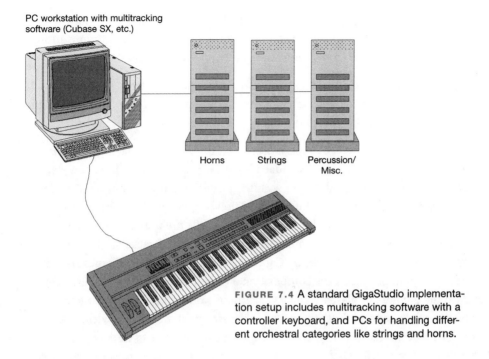

Horns   Strings   Percussion/
Misc.

FIGURE 7.4 A standard GigaStudio implementation setup includes multitracking software with a controller keyboard, and PCs for handling different orchestral categories like strings and horns.

Live Orchestras

I now move to a method of music production that lets you cut out the multipurpose option almost entirely: a live orchestra. Two orchestras that have been recorded on game soundtracks, Seattle's Northwest Sinfonia and the Salt Lake Symphony, are listed in the Fat Pipeline diagram (**Figure 7.1**). Live orchestras are becoming more popular in games for various reasons:

1   The orchestra in various forms (ensembles of four or so instruments to full-size orchestras of 20 to 60 or more instruments) is used in nearly 60 percent of all entertainment soundtracks, with electronica and bands making up the remaining 40 percent. Orchestras are used regularly in visual entertainment for presenting the widest variety of musical expression. This is now carrying over to games, since games are, after all, visual.

2   The orchestra is one of the most effective ways to express drama and emotion through music. In short, an orchestra still sounds damn good.

3 Major symphony orchestras such as the Los Angeles Film Players have special contracts that offer better rates for games. This makes it more affordable for developers to pursue the highest-quality live orchestral scores.

4 Overseas orchestras such as the Budapest Symphony offer lower fees than domestic orchestras do, making the use of an orchestra even more affordable and thus accessible to a wider range of game developers.

A live orchestra is a thrill to experience, especially when it is playing your own music. However, it also uses a standard instrument set and thus produces standard-sounding music (unless you wish the players to employ nonstandard playing techniques). Therefore, a lot of games flooding the market have soundtracks that are very similar to those of feature films. While the musical themes may be compelling, they are not as unique as the game soundtracks of old. For example, take the game *Strider* by Capcom, released in 1989. Its themes are brilliantly written but bear little compositional resemblance to most modern scores. Also the themes are played using FM synthesis rather than live instruments. Nevertheless, putting those themes to live instrumentation would yield a refreshingly masterful score. A new challenge facing composers is to find a unique way to use the orchestra to give games a unique sound. The answer is adaptive soundtracks, but that is a different topic altogether (see Chapter 4, "Design").

To achieve the majesty of an orchestra, many considerations (listed later in the pipeline) must be weighed. Make sure you have these ducks lined up before assuming that you'll be able to have James Horner happily conducting away within hours of calling him.

Crazy contracts

Contracts define your relationship with an orchestra. Yes, they're boring, but they'll also make your life far easier in the long run so you can concentrate on music rather than paperwork.

Some of the information listed here can also be found in *The Complete Guide to Game Audio,* by Aaron Marks, and if you're a member of the Game Audio Network Guild (www.audiogang.org), you can have access to sample contracts on its Web site.

If you are working for a publisher, find out whether the publisher has a legal department that handles contracts. If the publisher has not worked with an orchestra before, you may need to lend the legal department some help in terms of letting them know what to consider.

Rates

Like anything else that has a price, orchestra rates vary, but if you want to be realistic you should first consider your recording location. You should also consider the space you're recording in and the rental fee for that space, as well as the price for a recording engineer, a conductor, and a manuscript technician for preparing the sheet music. (Sometimes the conductor does this and is also the composer of the music.)

Europe: Recording orchestras is cheaper in Europe than in the United States. The Prague Symphony (which records in the Prague Ballroom) and the Budapest Symphony will work for around $400 to $800 per session depending on the number of musicians. A standard session is about 4 hours long and yields roughly 1 to 2 minutes of finished audio after editing and mastering are complete.

United States: The most inexpensive orchestra I know of in the States is the Austin Symphony in Texas. As of this writing, you can hire its players for $25 to $30 per hour each. A group of 30 musicians costs around $3600 for a 4-hour session, but the number of players can be cut in half and the musical parts doubled. (*Doubling* is a technique I cover later in this chapter, in the "Ensemble/Soloists" section.) The quality that results from doubling is excellent. Rates can go higher still: Members of the Los Angeles Philharmonic, for example, charge well over twice the amount for the Austin Symphony. Is the performance better for the money? In all honesty, that's hard to say unless you're a musician yourself, but the L.A. players are more practiced at playing for film and might be able to generate more emotion and depth. Let your ears be the judge.

Content

Everyone involved in the project should sign a contract, since a contract that applies to an entire orchestra may not be satisfactory for an individual. The process takes more time but is more thorough—and when it comes to the law and negotiations, one cannot be thorough enough. The following are the most important elements in a contract for session musicians and performers in an orchestra:

Nondisclosure agreement (NDA): Since the publisher owns every part of the game before it's even a game, it needs protection against any information being leaked out before the game is released. The NDA is usually a single page signed by every person involved with the orchestra, from the players to the engineering crew. Anyone who signs the NDA agrees to not mention anything concerning the project to outsiders or give away any materials related to the project.

Description of services: Outlining the deal is very important, especially to avoid loopholes. If the nature of the arrangement between the publisher and the performers is not outlined, a player can easily say, "You wanted me to play for 2 hours, yet we played for 3, so I'm charging you more money." Putting a cap on the amount of hours played or agreeing on a flat fee of some sort helps avoid additional charges. (Performers are typically paid by the hour and usually work for 4-hour blocks.)

Grant of rights: According to the law, when anything is created, the person creating it is also its owner unless a legal document states otherwise. In the case of an orchestra, once a player performs a piece, the publisher who is paying the player for it owns the recording of that piece.

A catch to this is that the player can charge additional money depending on how the recording is used. Someone who buys, say, a motorcycle can use it for any purpose, even for personal financial gain. The same isn't always true when a company buys a performance or a composition. If a game publisher uses the piece in a game as well as in an advertisement for that game, additional charges may be imposed for the advertisement. Often a publisher counters this by stating in the contract that every possible right in perpetuity is granted to the publisher upon the execution of the recording. Performers or composers can be prepared by stating in the contract that they will be paid additional money for any uses of their work beyond the game itself.

Limitation of liability: This is another protective measure for the publisher. In the past, without this protection, performers or anyone involved with a recording session could turn on the publisher in the event of injury or other bad circumstances that happened during the recording, demanding all kinds of compensation. If the publisher forgets to pay, deliberately doesn't pay, or takes a long time to pay for services rendered, additional money can be demanded. The limitation of liability clause thus "limits" what the publisher is "liable" for, and can include every possible situation where any kind of compensation can be demanded, including acts of God (also known as force majeure).

Let's move on to how to use the orchestra.

Soloists and ensembles

An option when using a live orchestra is to record a single instrument or a small ensemble of three to five players. A technique called *multiplying* enables a composer to record three French horns and create the impression that 20 are playing. In addition, a single voice or a lilting English horn solo might be just as effective at communicating a theme that may initially call for an entire string section.

Interview with Marty O' Donnell

Marty O' Donnell has created game music for some of the world's most popular titles, the latest being *Halo: Combat Evolved*, developed by Microsoft for its Xbox console. Having written numerous "jingle" scores for the advertisement industry in Chicago, he is well versed in the orchestral multiplying technique. I quiz him about it here:

AB: *How did you accomplish multiplying in your projects for O'Donnell/ Salvatori in Chicago?*

MO: I have continued to use that technique on most of my projects including *Halo* and *Halo 2*. I rarely record large groups. If I have a scratch track of a symphonic piece, I have string players come in and play along with it so I get a good basic idea of them playing through a full score. Then I go back in and start [multiplying] (in Chicago we called it "multing").

This technique began with vocalists. In fact, SAG [Screen Actors Guild] and AFTRA [American Federation of Television and Radio Artists] have a special part in their contract: If you are in a group of singers and decide to "mult," the rates go up and you get more money.

CONTINUED ▶

Interview with Marty O' Donnell, continued

There is also a difference between *sweetening* and *multing*. Multing means you sing or play the same part over again. Sweetening means "I sang the first tenor part the first time and I'm going to harmonize with myself." Those are actual union terms, so you get more if you're sweetening than if you're multing.

Because of those traditions in Chicago, you wouldn't go out and hire a 110-piece orchestra. You might hire 8 or 10 violins and have them play the divisi part, and you sweeten or mult them to sound like 16 or 20 players. You keep doing that until all the violin players have played all the parts, but you're only hiring eight players.

AB: *What instruments would you say can be multed most effectively?*

MO: The strings are the ones that [get this treatment] the most. You don't necessarily want two flutes playing in unison. You might as well have a first clarinet and second clarinet in harmony. Multing strings is the best way to thicken them up. In that process we would ask the players to "change up the vibrato" a little bit to get some variation from the first recording.

The minimum frame group is four violins, three cellos, and one viola. What you end up getting still doesn't sound like 80 strings, though, so if you have the money I'd recommend getting as many players as possible if you want a true, great, rich chorus and thickening effect.

Full orchestras

Using a full orchestra for game music is becoming more possible with the low rates that abound. It usually consists of a 40- to 60-piece set with first violins, second violins, violas, cello, flutes, clarinets, oboes, French horns, trumpets, bassoons, tubas, timpani, a harp, a snare, and a cymbal or tam-tam. The sound of a full orchestra is incomparable, so the price is worth it, even if only for a few minutes in the game.

Considerations for a full orchestra are different than those for a smaller ensemble, as the recording requirements are far more complex. Most orchestras have their own recording crew that will work for hourly fees similar to those of the players. You can save a great deal of time and effort if you set up the microphones and recording gear yourself; still, no one knows the acoustics and recording requirements of the space the players normally perform in better than the engineers that work full time with the orchestra. When in doubt, spend the money and use them.

A full orchestra requires a conductor, whereas an ensemble does not. You can hire the conductor, or you can use the composer if he or she is a trained conductor.

The musicians will need music to read, and an orchestrator can provide this music if the composer doesn't write music notation or isn't experienced with writing for a full score. If the composer can both conduct and provide the music, you save a great deal of time and money.

Licensing

Licensing music is now fairly standard among top-tier publishers. It differs from other methods because a publisher or developer buys the rights, usually from a music publisher, to license music that has already been written and/or performed. Marketing departments at game companies salivate over the cross-promotional opportunities that become available by using a top pop or rock act in conjunction with a game. However, this excitement is usually not born out of a love for game music as a whole or the desire to raise awareness of it. It's often simply another means to make money and gain recognition, created from greed. Sounds very hippieish of me to say, but it really is true.

In the "Bands and pop" section, I will explore the appropriate use of licensed music and how it can truly make a game shine, as opposed to tacking a popular name to a game to make it sell more copies. I'm not denying that money is a driving force in this industry. It's making money with careful planning and effective production methods that will result in creating better games.

Crazy contracts

I've discussed the use of contracts in regard to orchestras; it differs slightly with licensing. How the contract should be written depends on the following factors:

Popularity: The popularity of the artist from whom the game publisher wants to license the music relates directly to what it costs to use that music. The rate for licensing a song by a pop superstar can be as high as $50,000.

Grant of rights: Gaining the rights to use a song in any manner is much less likely to happen with licensed music. Record companies are masters of publishing rights and will most likely take a huge up-front fee for allowing a song or piece to be used in the game itself and nowhere else (unless the game developer is willing to pay another exorbitant sum).

Contract considerations for licensing and performance go beyond what I've described here. For example, organizations such as the American Society of Composers, Authors, and Publishers (ASCAP) and Broadcast Music Inc. (BMI) are devoted to allowing musicians to publish music and retain the rights to be paid when their music is used in all kinds of ways (such as being performed in public). These organizations normally function well in the record industry but are starting to wonder what to do about music published in games. Check out www.ascap.com and www.bmi.com for more details.

Additional information on contracts can be found in *All You Need to Know About the Music Business,* by Donald S. Passman.

Bands and pop

I'll continue with the sort of music that is licensed the most these days. The following acts have licensed their music for games; keep in mind that this list is far from complete, and I haven't heard music by half of these artists.

Accelerator	Epidemic	Michael Jackson	Phife Dawg
Andrew W.K.	Filter	Jimmy Eat World	Photek
Apollo 440	Flipswitch	Judas Priest	Prodigy
Audiovent	A Flock of Seagulls	Jurassic 5	Quarashi
Beck	Fluke	Kool & the Gang	Rush
Blondie	Foo Fighters	Lenny Kravitz	Saliva
Bon Jovi	Future Sound of London	Leftfield	Seether
David Bowie		Ludacris	Silverchair
Laura Branigan	Reeves Gabrels	Madonna	Lonnie Liston Smith
Bush	Peter Gabriel	MC Supernatural	Snoop Dogg
The Cardigans	Garbage	Method Man	Soul Coughing
The Chemical Brothers	Good Charlotte	Motley Crue	Source Direct
	Grandmaster Flash & the Furious Five	Mr. Mister	State of Shock
Cold		Nappy Roots	Stone Temple Pilots
The Crystal Method	Hall & Oates	OK Go	Uncle Kracker
The Cult	(hed) Planet Earth	Orbital	Underworld
Cutting Crew	Jimi Hendrix	Ozzy Osbourne	Whodini
Daft Punk	Irakere	Papa Roach	Rob Zombie
Dry Cell	Ivory Wire		

Ninety percent of the games that use music by these performers involve driving or sports. The remaining 10 percent largely include adventure and action games.

I will now examine the appropriateness of pop music for games. A pop artist writes a piece of music as an independent work of art; it almost never has anything to do with a game. Sometimes, however, the emotional theme of a pop song can reflect the emotional theme of a game. This is where marketing and licensing staff and game-music executives get their inspiration to link the song to the game.

Wipeout XL (**Figure 7.5**), released in 1996, featured tracks from groups that had exploded into the mainstream from the electronica genre. The United States had just hit a period in pop music in which there was a backlash against synthesizers after the overly campy, synthesizer-filled hits of the 1980s. The timing was perfect for a new kind of pop music to emerge in the early 1990s, and the result was what is now known as electronica.

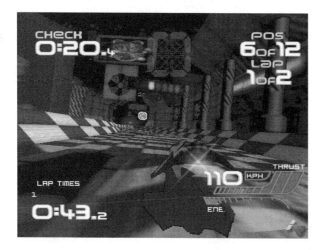

FIGURE 7.5 *Wipeout XL* is one of the best examples of a game with appropriately licensed music.

The timing was excellent too for *Wipeout XL* to include some of the best tracks from this avant-garde genre, because the game itself was so futuristic. The music was mostly instrumental, with few vocals to distract players. Some tracks were heavy and up-tempo and others were more subdued, but all the music suited the game as a whole. It was as though the music had been written specifically for the action: It was the first time people looked up and said, "Wow, this hit music *works* for this game."

Grand Theft Auto: Vice City (**Figure 7.6**) is a sequel to one of the best-selling games of all time: *Grand Theft Auto 3,* which enables players to do just about anything they want within the confines of a predetermined space. In *Vice City,* the space is Miami of a couple of decades ago, where players can freely drive around and commit crimes, receiving various rewards depending on the crime.

FIGURE 7.6 *Grand Theft Auto: Vice City* is a game in which the player can drive (or fly) around Miami in the 1980s.

While driving, the player can listen to a radio in their car, truck, or other vehicle (ambulances and police cars can be stolen, for example). The developer, Rockstar Games, licensed music by Madonna and Michael Jackson to help immerse the player in the 1980s, and the scheme was brilliant. The music was appropriate for the action and the time period, and the player could choose from a selection of radio stations.

Plenty of games use licensed music well, but others throw in licensed music just for the sake of marketing opportunities, or because an executive or manager wants their favorite band to play in their game, regardless of whether the music is appropriate. Some games even have music with vocals blaring when the player needs to hear important sonic feedback (such as characters speaking onscreen). So be wary, and think carefully about whether licensed music will work for your game's genre and design.

There is also a great opportunity to let licensed music change adaptively with gameplay. Titles such as Sony's *Frequency* and *Amplitude* use licensed pop songs in games where the player's goal is to mix and remix the parts of a particular song (such as bass, drums, harmony instrument, melody instrument, and voice) so that they play at once. This kind of integration can be done in more interesting ways with more conventional game genres. Imagine having drums in a pop song kick in when an action sequence begins.

Nonpop

In some cases, music that is not on the Top 40 charts is licensed. This occurs in roughly 40 to 50 percent of game music. A classic example is John Williams' *Star Wars* soundtrack, which is used in many LucasArts game titles set in the *Star Wars* universe. Another example is Midway's *MLB Slugfest: Loaded*, which uses "Wish I Never Met You" by the group State of Shock. Appropriate for a baseball game? You decide!

SFX

We now move on to sound effects. Fortunately, sound effects are much less complex in terms of production, but they are no less important than music; some would even say they're far more important.

Outsourced/in-house effects

You can acquire sound effects either from a sound effects house such as Soundelux or Danetracks (there are many multipurpose composers who also provide sound effects, and they're cheaper) or from an in-house sound designer. I personally prefer the latter. An in-house designer can be much more intimately linked with the production of a game, and the closer the designer is to production, the more accurate the sound effects will be. Music that generally fits the mood can work fine for a game, but sound effects that are even slightly off-kilter can ruin it.

Libraries/custom effects

Everything that goes into a sound effect is put together—mixed, equalized, and *effected* (applying effects such as reverb and delay)—in a multitrack program such as Nuendo or Cubase SX, but the raw sound material comes from one of two sources. One is a sound library available from a distributor such as Sound Ideas or Hollywood Edge. You'll find millions of sound effects that might be appropriate for what you need, and you can combine sounds to create anything that's not available. It's a spiffy method that's done at least half of the time in most game projects.

The other method, which is more difficult but potentially more satisfying, is to create sounds yourself. Use a recording system such as a DAT recorder, a Sony MiniDisc recorder, or a portable digital recorder (storage media is usually in the form of a memory card or a hard drive) to strike out into the underbrush or the local meat-packing plant—anywhere you think you might get a usable recording. If you have a recording studio or even a halfway quiet room in your house, you can record custom sounds there, too. For a wealth of information on recording custom sounds, visit `http://filmsound.studienet.org`.

Interactive Mixing Fully Realized

Once you get your beautiful sounds and music on the hard drives you're using for your project, the time comes to actually integrate them into the game, just as a sound engineer does during the postproduction of a film. This is where technology and production intertwine a bit. I'm discussing interactive mixing in this chapter on production because it involves the use of special technology to produce better audio within the game itself, and therefore is considered part of the production chain.

As I mentioned earlier, a film-sound engineer handles recordings for use in a film (music, sound, dialogue) and mixes them together with the film itself so that they not only are timed properly, but also sound good to the ear and are integrated contiguously. (Voice is usually given a slightly higher volume than music and sound, as it is usually more important to the presentation of a story.) In games, this kind of mixing is being done more and more, as music, sound, and voice for games are becoming more similar to those of film.

Why isn't this process in the Fat Pipeline? Excellent question. For all the possibilities provided by the multipurpose, orchestra, and licensed music options, *none* of them offers specialized interactive mixing. This is going to change gradually, since composers and engineers—who want the music to show up properly in the game itself—know more about making it sound good than the programmers on the game team do. But at the moment, this kind of mixing work needs to be done within the game environment itself. This isn't so much of a problem for PC games, except for security—if a freelance multipurpose composer or sound designer receives a prerelease version of the game, what's to stop them from distributing it? For console games, the person doing the mixing would need development hardware that costs thousands of dollars, and most developers are loath to part with that kind of money.

Editing on the Fly

In the 1980s, game developers gave programmers sounds, music, and voice to integrate. That is, the programmer simply "hooked" these elements to events or objects in the game. The integration process is a little more complex now. Here's why.

If you listen to certain games today, you can hear a drastic volume difference between sound effects and music. That was not always the case. Listen to the 1985 arcade game *The Legend of Kage,* for example, and you will hear an upbeat pop soundtrack that reflects the progress of the ninja character, which you control by throwing ninja stars and swiping with your mighty blade any foe who opposes you. Unfortunately, while this music is going on you also hear sound effects that are about twice as loud, including deafening thunderclaps and ear-piercing clangs that ring out when an enemy blocks your sword attacks. While in most games, sound effects are more important than music for player feedback and interaction, the sound effects drown out the music in this case. Better mixing would have solved this problem.

Not too long after *The Legend of Kage* hit the arcades, the game industry recognized this problem. In response, game developers began including a cursory pass at mixing during sound production.

Mixing began in one of two inefficient and time-consuming ways. In the first, a sound designer or composer provided a programmer with a piece of music, a vocal sample, or a sound effect, and the programmer integrated it in code. If the volume was too high, the sound designer or composer changed the volume and sent it back to the programmer. The programmer integrated it, and the entire process repeated until the sound was satisfactory.

In the other method of correcting sound, voice, or music, a sound designer or composer (or sometimes a programmer) changed settings within the code itself or a text file associated with the code. You can imagine how annoying that task was, but interestingly enough, the people who did it got so used to it that they actually preferred doing it that way!

In the making of *Deus Ex: Invisible War,* the process was more up-to-date: The QA team reported a sound as being too loud, too soft, audible through a solid steel wall, and the like. The audio team then adjusted the volume and activated a process called *rebuilding.* The audio team then added the adjusted volume to a master *build,* or current collection of game content and code. Between 30 and 60 minutes later, the QA team could retest the volume with the changes the audio team made.

Today's methods are much more sophisticated, but the idea is simple: If a sound doesn't work in the game for some reason—the volume is too low, the treble or bass needs tweaking, or the sound itself needs to be replaced—you can change the sound's properties *while the game is running.* It cuts out the programmer from the process and allows changes to occur in real time without having to wait for any kind of rebuilding or compiling of code.

The Unreal Engine, Renderware Studio, and many proprietary engines are starting to support features that will allow for this interactive mixing. As I've mentioned in earlier chapters, the PlayStation 2 has a tool called Scream (Scriptable Engine for Audio Manipulation), and the Xbox has one called Xact (Xbox Audio Content Tool). In the future these tools will become not just optional but standard, and the job of interactive mixing will become standard practice as well. There may also be companies and contractors that will specialize in integrating *middleware* tools—software tools that provide functionality but do not constitute a complete game engine—into game engines and proprietary systems. Such a middleware tool could be a custom game engine that's linked to specific platforms, such as only the Xbox and the PC.

The Tail End of Production

In game development today, there is no time in the schedule devoted to audio mastering, mixing, and postproduction the way there is with films. Films require that the visuals be complete before sound and music are mixed with them, because if the visuals change in any way after the music and sound are mixed, the components would not match and would thus be confusing and jarring to watch.

The same applies to games, but schedules are at the point where art, design, and programming details are changed right up until the game is scheduled to ship. Eventually a postproduction cycle will be incorporated, but until then, the audio team must begin production as early as possible so that by the time the game hits *alpha* (the phase at which all content in the game is complete), as much integration work as possible has been done.

This leaves room just for fixing problems, which is essentially what postproduction is.

Metrics Tools

Fixing problems can be done only if you can identify them in the first place. While developing *Deus Ex: Invisible War,* we were lucky to have a programmer dedicated to spotting problems and gathering information about them while the game was played. His task was creating tools to gather this information, also known as *metrics.*

One metrics tool helped us find out how many times a sound was played during any period of time or in any particular instance. So, for example, if the sound of a buzzing fluorescent light played an inordinate number of times in a level (say, 1 million times in 1 hour), the metrics tool would report it and we could look into why it was occurring. The reason, as it turned out, was that the buzzing sound was being triggered by the code at the same time the lightbulb flickered, and the flicker occurred thousands of times in a given gameplay period.

In other cases, sounds were played at inappropriate times and actually generated other sounds that didn't appear to mesh with the rest of the mix. Our physics system that controlled the impact of human bodies, for example, sometimes registered the impact of a limb or head on the ground hundreds of times and triggered the generated sound the same number of times. We weren't sure which part of the body was doing this until the metrics tool told us, which helped tremendously in troubleshooting the problem.

Metrics tools can also be retrofitted for audio purposes directly, such as performing a *spectrum analysis* on a specified time period of gameplay. A spectrum analysis is a digital representation, usually in a line chart or graph, of the frequencies that are played within a specified period of time. They're helpful in observing if there is too much bass or treble in that time period. The engineers can then adjust the frequencies if they're proving to be annoying or inconsistent to the ear.

CHAPTER 8
Ideal Technology

Technology is the foundation of a game. Some game developers have used technological breakthroughs in areas such as graphics and user interface as marketing bait, and have been very successful at it. However, to create a genuinely good game, the development team marries the design to the technology so that the two work together as an efficient machine. We can see examples of this in LucasArts games such as *The Dig*, whose design uses the iMUSE system to determine how the music will play. Check out Chapter 7, "Ideal Production," for more details.

Such design-technology relationships are great examples of how to move forward, but given how rapidly game design changes, it's difficult to maintain the use of one technology pool for long. Therefore we progress by defining ideal technological functionality in an audio system that retains essential functions but has the ability to be expanded and modified as well. This chapter is devoted to identifying these essential functions and defining expandability. After all, if you're reading this you no doubt want to be the leader of the pack. Simply plugging in music and sound effects is such a tiny piece of games' technological puzzle—if you want to impress everyone you'll know how to put together the whole thing.

As I mentioned in Chapter 7, gone is the old method of giving your assets to a programmer to plug them in, praying that they'll show up in the game nice and neat and sounding great. The sound folk wanted responsibility; well, now they've got it. This scares the hell out of the more artistic of us, but it's still a much better approach than making programmers do the work.

We audio developers have been thrown into a world where we're expected to understand principles that are completely alien to us. It's like we're learning to play a new instrument, and it's quite frightening. However, this world invites us just as it invites any programmer. It challenges us to think according to concepts we never imagined and mold our art in ways we couldn't conceptualize. Some people have bravely trod forward and have discovered, with great joy, new means of creative expression such as adaptive soundtracks. Some people have chosen to stick to producing music, sound, and voice. The latter is just as noble a choice as the former.

Let me tell you, though, that if you want your music to be experienced in a completely different way—so that some 8-year-old's eyes widen to the size of dinner plates because of the music's genius—understanding how to integrate your audio assets into the game is the way to do it. I just finished playing the first level of *Thief: Deadly Shadows,* and its sound was great. It got that way because its audio director, Eric Brosius, insisted on having complete control of integrating the audio. With this in mind, I now dive into the great ocean of game-audio integration.

Integration DPM

I explained the power of a development process map (DPM) in Chapter 1. In this chapter I approach the DPM from the perspective of integration: the nitty-gritty of how sound, music, and voice are hooked into the game. Integration is important because actually writing music means nothing if the music cuts off when the player enters a conversation or if the music doesn't loop properly. Integration can also make the music play adaptively—that is, change according to player actions. Let's explore the fundamentals. Take a look at the integration DPM (**Figure 8.1**).

Integration DPM

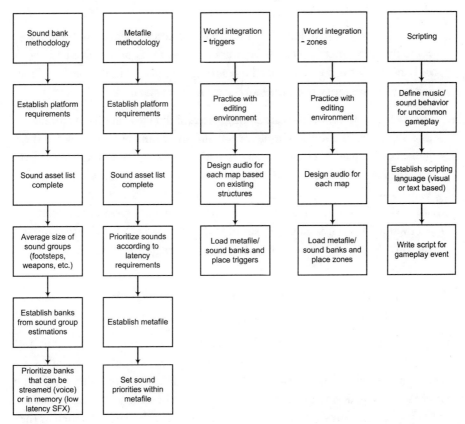

FIGURE 8.1 This integration DPM shows all aspects of how sound, music, and voice are hooked into the game.

File Management

Your first decision must be how to organize all the files in the game. Each file represents an asset, whether a sound effect, music, or a voice-over line. The most important consideration in organizing files is the platform on which you will be developing, because different platforms handle files in different ways. First, however, let's look at the ground rules that apply to all platforms:

▶ Each sound file is like an audio CD. You typically store CDs somewhere different from where you play them. Sound files are stored with the rest of the game's data—usually on a hard drive, a CD, or a DVD.

▶ For the sound files to play, they must be moved out of storage to a location that is able to play them—the equivalent of the audio device on which you play your CDs.

▶ The fastest way to play sound files is usually to access them from memory: Random access memory can have sounds placed in it and removed; read-only memory cannot be changed once things are placed in it. The entire file is copied to memory from the storage area, then activated.

▶ A slower way to play files is streaming. Streaming takes data from storage and copies small chunks of a file into RAM one chunk at a time. When the game code triggers a chunk of data to play, that data is removed from RAM and the next chunk is lined up behind it to play immediately afterward. Understandably, this process is slower. Imagine if the first 30 seconds of a song were on one CD and you had to swap it out for a second disc when you wanted to hear the next 30 seconds. The process of playing a streamed file isn't this cumbersome, but it does take longer to initially load the file for playback.

The two most effective ways of organizing sounds based on platform are sound banks and metafiles.

As of this writing, the platform that has been around the longest and is still in current development is the PlayStation 2. Compared with the Xbox and GameCube consoles, it has the smallest amount of RAM and the least processing power that can be devoted to audio. As I explain in the next section, it is necessary to use sound banks with this platform as well as with platforms such as the Nintendo GameCube and on portable devices such as the Game Boy Advance.

Why continue to develop on the PS2 if it lags so far behind? There are more than 60 million PS2 units in the United States, and the platform has a large market share. Also, just because a platform isn't on the cutting edge of technology doesn't mean great games can't be developed for it. Besides, the next revision of gaming hardware is always around the corner—the PlayStation 3 isn't far off.

Sound Bank Methodology

The way you organize a game's files depends primarily on the platform on which you're developing. For the PlayStation 2, a sound designer or composer saves the files in *sound banks* before the sound engine code loads them into the game's memory. Sound banks are groups of sounds that you can organize however you want. I'll get into the details of sound objects, or "containers," in the next section, but for now think of a sound bank as a box in which you organize sounds. Why use banks in the first place? Why not allow access to all the files at once? Because all the files together would take up too much space to be stored in the PlayStation 2's memory. To make things easier, banks are used to load into RAM only the files that need to make sounds at the point in the game the player is actually playing. Sounds that don't occur until later in the game are kept in storage (on a hard drive for the Xbox, a CD for a PC. and a DVD for all platforms except the GameCube).

Before you bank sounds, you should know the requirements of your platform. On the PlayStation 2, sound data is limited to about 2 MB of RAM. This means that no matter what, no more than 2 MB of sound can be played back at the same time. This is fairly constricting, especially for the parts of the game where you want a lot of sounds to play at once.

Once you have an idea of what sounds will be required, you can establish how many sounds will play back at once by reading the game's design document. This document explains what sounds are needed and when, and you use it to fill out your sound asset spreadsheet. You can also use the asset list to specify which sounds go into which banks. For example, suppose that when a player in the game uses a particular weapon, the game engine code swaps the sounds the weapon makes with those of another weapon (each weapon sound set being represented in a bank). The audio engineer can glean this from the design doc when he reads "Player 1 can switch between weapons." You'll use this kind of information as a basis for organizing banks.

Next, ask the lead programmer what bank size would work best for the game. This is an important task that can be included in the "Define platforms" section of the audio DPM, under "Buffer size/priority scheme." A buffer is the amount of memory needed to load a bank of sound effects. This will vary based on what the sound engine is doing, such as streaming or prioritizing (both of which I'll cover shortly). Most of the time programmers are comfortable with a bank size much smaller than 2 MB. This is because a bank represents sounds loaded according to priority. For example, if a player is using one weapon at a time in an action game and all the weapon sounds are in one bank, the unused weapon sounds are taking up memory that could be used for other things such as environmental sound effects or voice. Using smaller banks gives greater control because it is a more efficient use of RAM, and it lets you prioritize groups of sounds at different points in the game according to the importance of playback. For example, sounds like voice are more important than distant explosions, and a bank system can reflect this priority. Then, you might ask, why not just have one bank for each sound and prioritize sounds individually? The answer to this is CPU processing time: It would be too costly for the CPU to prioritize each sound in and out of memory. Each file takes a bit of processing power to load; when many are loading at once, processing power is eaten up quickly, leaving little room for other components such as graphics.

Here's an example of a sound bank structure for a PlayStation 2 football game (**Figure 8.2**). Note that the compressed files are about one-fourth the size of the uncompressed files.

	A	B	C	D	E
	Bank Name / files	**Bank size**	**Bank size (compressed)**		
2	Footsteps	1280k	320k		
3	QuarterbackWalk1.wav	15k	3.75k		
4	QuarterbackWalk2.wav	20k	6.6k		
5	QuarterbackWalk3.wav	22k	5.5k		
6	QuarterbackWalk4.wav	23k	5.75k		
7	QuarterbackWalk5.wav	18k	6k		
8	etc..	etc..	etc..		
9					
10	Crowd cheers	500k	125k		
11	SoftMurmur.wav	40k	10k		
12	MediumMurmur.wav	38k	9.5k		
13	LoudMurmur.wav	52k	13k		
14	GoalCheerSoft.wav	58k	14.5k		
15	GoalCheerMedium.wav	91k	22.75k		
16	etc..				

ExampleBankStructure.xls

FIGURE 8.2
This sound bank structure for a PlayStation 2 football game show how banks are constructed and what the relative file sizes are.

In the case of a PlayStation 2's sound memory structure, sound data is usually compressed to one-quarter of its original size using a format called VAG. You can use Sony's proprietary program for developers, VagEdit, to convert your WAV files into VAG files. This is a great way to combat that 2 MB limitation for memory space on the PlayStation 2.

Let's take this a step further and add to the bank structure that list of priorities we talked about earlier (**Figure 8.3**).

	A	B	C	D	E	F
	Bank name / files	Bank size	Bank size (compressed)			Bank priority
2	Footsteps	1280k	320k			Used only during scrimmages.
3	QuarterbackWalk1.wav	15k	3.75k			
4	QuarterbackWalk2.wav	20k	6.6k			
5	QuarterbackWalk3.wav	22k	5.5k			
6	QuarterbackWalk4.wav	23k	5.75k			
7	QuarterbackWalk5.wav	18k	6k			
8	etc..	etc..	etc..			
9						
10	Crowd cheers	500k	125k			Used during gameplay. Not used for menus.
11	SoftMurmur.wav	40k	10k			
12	MediumMurmur.wav	38k	9.5k			
13	LoudMurmur.wav	52k	13k			
14	GoalCheerSoft.wav	58k	14.5k			
15	GoalCheerMedium.wav	91k	22.75k			
16	etc..					
17						
18						
19						

FIGURE 8.3 This sound bank structure shows bank priorities added.

As you can see, the "Bank priority" column tells the programmer that the banks can be loaded at certain points in the game. Having the priority listed in the bank structure list (which can double as an asset list) ensures that the sound team and programming team are aware of what sounds will be played and when.

Now we have our sound asset list, our bank structure, and our priorities. What are we missing? Remember how all platforms provide the option to stream as well as to use memory? Adding streaming as an option is the final step in prioritizing our files. Take a look at the finishing touch, the Streamed check box, in our bank management spreadsheet (**Figure 8.4**). Also note that if streaming isn't chosen, memory must be used to load the sound. These two methods are important to prioritize with the following information in mind: It takes longer to load files that are streamed from something like a DVD than it does to load files that are in RAM. The length of time it takes to load a file to play is called *latency* (as you may remember from the DPM). For example, music files don't usually need to be triggered as instantly as does a weapon sound that needs to be linked to a visual event like the firing of a gun. To keep this latency down, weapon sounds are prioritized to RAM, and music is prioritized to streaming.

	A	B	C	D	E	F	G	H	I
	Bank name / files	Bank size	Bank size (compressed)			Bank priority / instance	Streamed		
2	Footsteps	1280k	320k			Used only during scrimmages.			
3	QuarterbackWalk1.wav	15k	3.75k				☐		
4	QuarterbackWalk2.wav	20k	6.6k				☐		
5	QuarterbackWalk3.wav	22k	5.5k				☐		
6	QuarterbackWalk4.wav	23k	5.75k				☐		
7	QuarterbackWalk5.wav	18k	6k				☐		
8	etc.	etc.	etc.				☐		
9									
10	Crowd cheers	500k	125k			Used during gameplay. Not used for menus.			
11	SoftMurmur.wav	40k	10k				☐		
12	MediumMurmur.wav	38k	9.5k				☐		
13	LoudMurmur.wav	52k	13k				☐		
14	GoalCheerSoft.wav	58k	14.5k				☐		
15	GoalCheerMedium.wav	91k	22.75k						
16	etc.								
17									

FIGURE 8.4 The sound bank structure has a streaming option added as a check box.

Now we're now ready for integration.

Metafile Methodology

The PC and the Xbox offer different ways of handling files. Because more memory can be allocated to sound, a programmer may opt to use a *metafile* to store sounds. A metafile is simply a file containing a lot of other files that oftentimes are compressed, much like a ZIP file.

The sound designer or the composer uses this metafile to store *all* the sounds in the game. Here's how.

Establishing your platforms, as we have seen with sound banks in the DPM, is the first step when taking the metafile approach. If you're working with platforms that have a great deal of available RAM, using metasounds is a good idea because more sounds can be loaded into memory and then easily removed according to priority. With less RAM, organizing sounds into groups such as banks is much easier to deal with because there is less overhead. For example, when loading sounds with a bank structure, a single set of code instructions is all that is required to prioritize which sounds are used (for example, specific weapon groups). With metafiles, more code instructions must be used to determine whether each file playing is of higher priority than other sounds. These instruction codes can be kept to a minimum with banks (on a PlayStation 2, for instance) and need not be worried about on an Xbox using metafiles.

Once you've determined your platform requirements, you then need to create your sound asset list (again as you can see in the DPM).

As a data structure (which I define in the next section), a metafile is much easier for a composer or sound designer to deal with since you don't need to consider what sounds go where: They all go in one place. Therefore, to the sound designer or composer, a metafile appears just the same as a directory structure does somewhere like Windows Explorer. Doesn't that rock? With all this techno jargon, if I didn't say that once in a while I'd go out of my mind.

Assigning Priorities

Now that we've looked at two ways of organizing files on our DPM, the third and final task is to assign priorities to the sounds in the asset list.

With a metafile methodology, the sound designer can prioritize sounds individually. For example, a "wind" ambient loop can take higher priority than a "creaking tree" ambient loop if the platform determines that too many sounds are being played at any particular time; it can then drop the creaking tree ambient loop out of memory, that sound will stop playing, and the wind sound can continue playing.

With a sound bank methodology, the sound designer can prioritize sounds according to banks, meaning that a high-priority bank will play all the time no matter what and never be dropped out of memory, and a lower-priority bank will be dropped if higher-priority banks are being played simultaneously.

Both of these methodologies allow different ways to specify priority; the best way to do it for metafiles is within your sound-object editor (described in the next section). The specification for individual sound priority can range from 1 to x, 1 being the highest and x being the lowest. The audio team can determine this range, which will vary depending on the title. For sound banks, the best way to assess priorities is to send a programmer a list of the banks with the priority listed next to them.

Before I continue with the rest of the integration DPM, I must explain a few concepts about how files are organized to further illustrate the kind of advanced thinking going on in audio file management. It's important to understand these new ideas, as they promote better organization of game-audio assets. The bigger games grow, the more organized we need to be in handling the audio that goes into them. It has become a skill set unto itself that, if mastered, cuts development time by an average of at least 25 percent.

Easy Hookup

To organize your audio files well, you need to grasp how to integrate audio assets—that is, taking that beloved music, sound, and voice and making it all play back at the appropriate places in the game.

Abstract data types

The online encyclopedia Wikipedia defines *abstract data types* as "data types described in terms of the operations they support—their interface—rather than how they are implemented" (`http://en.wikipedia.org/wiki/Abstract_data_type`). I'll try to explain it in a slightly cozier way.

A lesson I learned only recently is that understanding abstract data types (data being anything that is processed by the game engine, such as music or sound) is a good idea. I had already learned this in high school in an advanced placement computer science course but didn't think about it much. I was too interested in girls at the time and barely scraped by with a D, but I still remember what data types are and why they are used. Above all, I learned that understanding them isn't rocket science, and it isn't just for geeks.

Sounds Within Containers

If you imagine a sound effect as an object such as a box, you can also imagine it as something that can interact with (and be influenced by) other things, like other boxes. At first this is a difficult concept to grasp, but it gets easier when presented in visual form with a story attached to it.

In this illustration (**Figure 8.5**), sound is no longer intangible or invisible; it is a box. Like a Palm handheld, the box has various capabilities. The Palm lets you write, draw, and—depending on what expansion cards it has—use it as a phone or a music player. The sound initially has simple attributes like pitch and volume, but depending on the expansion cards, it can be randomized or played with envelopes that affect its pitch and/or volume over time.

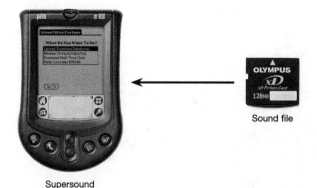

Supersound

Sound file

FIGURE 8.5 Imagine a sound as an object that can be placed into other objects and given attributes, in the way a card is placed into a Palm device and given its own properties.

Let's call our sound a *supersound*. I know it sounds corny, but it's original; the term *metasound* has been used. In fact, there really is no standard naming convention for this. (David Javelosa, ex-Sega sound designer and composer, tried to create a lexicon of terminology for all game-audio professionals, and it's high time we tried to complete this goal of solidifying our specialized vernacular.)

With its powers and functions in place, the supersound needs to be manipulated in some way. I'll begin by giving the supersound a name: Footstep. I have said the supersound is a box for good reason: The box can store things inside it.

Imagine you need to place footsteps in a game. The series of footsteps clearly needs to comprise more than one sound in order to avoid sounding repetitive and annoying. Let's say you have five different footstep sounds for a character. If you wanted to turn down the volume for all five footsteps, you would need to edit each footstep file individually. Doesn't sound like much fun, does it?

A better idea is to place all five files into a container—a supersound—and when an attribute (such as the volume) of that overall container is changed, the attributes of each file within the container are also changed. This is where the box becomes a "superbox," controlling the functionality of our supersounds. In other words, a sound file goes into a container (metasound) that can contain many files of the same type (for instance, a Footstep1-5.wav file inside the Footstep metasound). That container, or metasound, goes in yet another container, a metafile, which controls the properties of all the metasounds. In a UI interface, if you click a metasound, all the same property options will be listed.

Now let's picture a process where we use these powerful data types with the data we create inside them (see **Figure 8.6**).

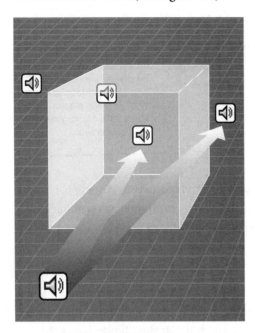

Sound Data Type Workflow

A) Sound files are placed inside super-sounds (example: Footstep sounds 1 through 5 are placed in Supersound 1).

B) Sound files can be given attributes through the supersounds (example: Footstep sounds 1 through 5 can be randomized).

C) Sound files are placed within a super-box and organized according to type. The superbox contains all supersounds in the game.

FIGURE 8.6 A superbox holds supersounds inside it; here is an example of an integration process workflow for sound data.

1   A sound is created. The sound is happy, but it could be better off with superpowers.

2   The sound needs to be placed in its superbox and given attributes to become a supersound. To do this, a programmer creates a tool called a *superbox*. An audio integrator, sound designer, or composer loads up this tool to work on the sound and give it properties, and can then add the sound to a master list. The audio integrator can do this with any other sounds that are created.

3   The master list is organized according to a directory structure. This structure lets sound integrators organize the sounds much as they would like them organized on their own computer, except they exist in the game code already. The programmer can sit back and relax at this point, at least when it comes to coding more audio integration.

4   The audio integrator takes this master list and opens a supersound. A window displays one or more individual sound files, and a single page within this window lists the attributes of the sound files. If the audio integrator wishes to edit a sound file within the supersound, all she has to do is click that file. To edit all sound files, all she has to do is select all the files and make the change.

The Object-Oriented Virtual Studio

The method for assigning sounds to data types, called *object-oriented development,* has been in use for some time to help folks understand how elements in a game (such as assets like artwork and sounds) work in a simpler way.

The environment for our object-oriented development is the superbox. Once you have that, all you need is a way to connect the supersounds and superboxes and their attributes to the game. You do this by adding the superbox to the same editing environment the game designers use. The game designers will use this environment to create the space in which the game will take place—whether a football stadium, a fighting arena, or an entire planet in a fantasy realm.

The sound integrator will load the superbox as well as the particular gameplay environment—also called the map or level—that you're working in. For a change of pace from the role-playing games I've given as examples so far, let's say you're working on a football game.

There are three main kinds of audio integration through this graphical user interface for level building that has just been described: world (environmental), character/object, and scripted. I'll start with world audio integration.

World Audio Integration

So, there it is: the stadium in all its glory sitting before you. What on earth are you supposed to do now? You should know how to work your way around the level-editing environment. A level editor within a typical game engine like Unreal or Renderware works by allowing the audio integrator to run around in the environment as the way the player would in the game itself. But for ease of editing and viewing, this editing environment will have three axes of view as well as a three-dimensional view of the environment (as seen in Chapter 4, "Design"). Scrolling around in this environment will get you accustomed to navigating properly, a skill that is vital for fast integration. Editing in this world is similar to the way you zoom in and out of audio files when you're editing them, but the world is in three dimensions instead of two.

After you get the hang of moving around in your game environment, it's time to integrate sounds and music. Load up your superbox GUI and click a sound in your directory structure.

At this point you have the ultimate feeling of power. As the audio integrator, you have now supplanted the programmer, and the power is in your hands to integrate sound. It's a fun power, but it isn't easy. We'll break it down to make it more chewable.

Zones and triggers

Currently the two most effective ways to integrate world audio are *triggers* and *zones.*

Triggers are points the audio integrator places in a map to designate locations where different sounds or music are activated or deactivated. In other words, a trigger is a switch to turn sounds on and off, fade sounds in and out, continue the playback of an existing audio file, play a sound that occurs only once when the trigger is activated, and so on.

The sounds that are controlled with triggers are often stereo sounds. Stereo is used for such effects as music and ambient (atmospheric) sounds, which don't require placement in a 3D map. Sounds controlled by triggers appear as small colored dots or icons in the editing space and have a radius of effect around them that usually is not represented visually. For example, you might place a trigger at the entrance to a hallway and another trigger at the opposite end. One trigger, when stepped on by the player, activates an ambient sound that plays and loops until the same trigger is stepped on again or the other trigger is stepped on. The sound then either switches to a new sound, with cross fades or another sound inserted as a transition, or it stops.

Triggers are useful for defining all kinds of ambient sound behaviors within the space of a map. But at times you may want sounds to play or stop playing in spaces that aren't defined by map boundaries—in the case of a stadium, perhaps various points on the field. In such cases, defining areas becomes more difficult without visual representation, and that's where zones come in.

Zones are objects the audio integrator places in a map to designate areas where sound plays or does not play. Say, for example, you have a stadium and you want crowd noise to fill a certain area. You click a button designated for creating sound zones, and a cube or pyramid (or another shape of your choice) appears that you can resize and move wherever you like. Right-clicking the cube lets you specify a sound (or supersound) that plays inside it.

Zones let you create arbitrary areas of sound in levels already defined by things the game designers have created—in this case, a stadium. This saves you the time of placing multiple triggers and worrying that a player might step in the assigned trigger radius. The drawback to a zone is that it is most useful for ambient sounds that loop and not much more. A trigger is better for implementing a one-shot sound (a sound that plays only once after the player activates it).

Character/Object Audio Integration

You can make crowds cheer and PA system music blare anywhere in your environment, but objects inside it with complex behaviors (like the football players) require a different approach. The game environment contains characters such as the player character (PC) and nonplayer characters (NPCs); objects can include a boulder that rolls down a hill (old game developers might recall the arcade classic *Krull*), a lightning bolt, and, in the case of our football example, a PA system speaker.

How do you integrate character sounds? By using the same editor you use to integrate world sounds. This is the preferred way to go, since characters end up in the environment. Here's how it works, ideally:

1   Load an interface window in your map editor that allows you to view PC or NPC animations.

2   Select the character you want. Characters are usually represented by a directory tree structure similar to that of Windows Explorer. The character's animations should appear.

3   Select the animation you want to look at. You should see the character in a display window with controls beneath the character for playing the animation, pausing it, and stopping it; you'll also see a slider to move from frame to frame in the animation. An indicator shows the animation's frame number while the animation is playing or stopped.

4 Beneath the controls you'll see a place to load sound files from your sound bank or metafile (containing your supersounds and superboxes) that you currently have loaded.

5 When you're at the frame of the animation for which you want a sound to be triggered, load a sound file from your metafile or sound bank. The sound will now play when that frame is played.

Yes, ladies and gentlemen, it's that simple! You can use this method to attach sounds to any character animations. This applies to actions from attacks to footsteps.

For objects, you should see a similar interface window with a directory tree structure. Integrating sounds into objects has a few additional rules (see the list that follows). If you don't care whether an object makes an ambient sound, skip that step and move on to something else. But don't blame me if you don't win an Audio of the Year award and the guy who did read that item does.

1 Objects are often separated into different *classes,* or types. For example, a door is in a different class than a lightning bolt effect (effects are also known as *particles*).

2 Different objects work differently in terms of sound. A door may not have an animation showing it opening and closing. The action of opening and closing the door may be controlled within the game's code rather than by way of an editable user interface. However, the display window should let you see the door opening and closing exactly the way it does in the game, and a timer should indicate how long it takes in seconds and milliseconds. This allows you to create a sound timed perfectly to the action of the object.

3 The same rules apply to a lightning bolt; just because an animation isn't present for the bolt in its own display window doesn't mean you can't see it in the game and assign a sound to it. Remember also that each class may have editable variations; each lightning bolt in the game may not behave the same way. Each *instance* of the lightning bolt class therefore has its own settings stored in the same location as the original class (think of the original as a template). So when you click LightningBolt, as it may be displayed in the window, you see not only the original class but also each instance, and then can assign sounds accordingly.

4   When multiple-class instances—if there are 20 kinds of lightning bolts, for example, all with different timings—demand more sounds than you can store in memory, you can edit metasounds to follow instances of classes that vary. This means you can set a single sound effect to play perfectly with each lightning bolt instance using an effect known as *time shift,* which lengthens or shortens the sound without changing its pitch (if your game/sound engine supports this function).

In this game, characters and objects made sounds of appropriately varying volumes when the player was farther away or closer, but there were only sequential volume shifts as you changed distance. The volume level shifted by increments of about 6 dB to 7 dB. The point at which the human ear can discern a shift in volume is a decrease or increase of around 2 dB to 3 dB—but the game, because of memory restrictions as well as movement distances (all characters moved in increments or *blocks* of 10 feet), allowed for only about five volume levels. In a nutshell, when an enemy creature was two blocks away, it sounded almost half as loud as it did when it was one block away. When the creature was fairly close, it made a noticeable noise, but when it was right next to you, the noise was so loud it was startling. There was no ramping of volume between the two blocks.

Scripting Integration

Scenes that don't happen often in a game require scripting. To understand how to integrate scripting, let's think of a scene involving something beyond basic gameplay mechanics such as attacking, or in the case of a football game, the quarterback passing the ball. Here's an example of a football game situation that requires more than a single action and is more emotionally driven than something done as a matter of course throughout the game:

> **NOTE** When the player executes a perfect red blitz move in this football game, I want the running back to automatically defend himself against any blockers. This is a hard move to execute, so once the player is in control of the running back, he can head straight for the end zone. Musically, something special should happen while the running back is blazing his trail. There should be a victory theme of some sort played with emotionally charged, upbeat sounds and rhythms, but the piece should also build. When the running back reaches the end zone, the piece should seamlessly transition into a climax touchdown theme.

What I've described here is often referred to as a *scripted event*. It doesn't happen often, so it requires special code. In a 3D first-person adventure game, a scripted event can help drive the story forward and is often a cut scene with conversations and action that doesn't otherwise happen during gameplay.

In the football game example above, the code that controls this scripted event can be contained in the code seen only by programmers or be described in a special script interface within the editor we're familiar with. For the scene I've described, this script interface uses a "middle ground" language between the English words in the description above and the code language (such as Visual C++) used in the rest of the game. This is the script itself. Head here to see examples of scripts in action and more information on how to use them:

```
http://msdn.microsoft.com/library/default.asp?url=/library/en-us/dmus-
prod/htm/scriptdesigner.asp
```

The point is that you should be able to link your music to *anything* in the game, and with scripting language you can bypass programmers. Scripting allows the audio integrator to generate more complex and intricate audio behaviors with minimal aid from programmers, and as such it gives a great deal of satisfying creative freedom to the audio team as a whole.

The ideal in this situation is to give the scripting interface more recognizable language in the event nonprogrammers want to change what's happening in the scripted event. While computers use more concise language than do humans to describe actions they perform—and the conforming of computer language to human language is a subject best left to scholars for the future—we can try to bridge the gap in the meantime. With knowledge of the syntax, an audio integrator can recognize the following script more easily than Visual C++ code (used by most programmers), and the compiler (the software that takes code and translates it to binary language that the computer processes) can also recognize it. Here's an example of a script.

Script Red Blitz

This script uses very crude logic, but let's take a look at it. It's pretty easy to understand once you know what it's describing (that is, the scripted sequence described in English earlier in this section).

```
<Begin Script RedBlitz>
<Scrimmage>=Execute
Wait[Up_Up_Left_RightTrigger+LeftTrigger]
<Control>=RunningBack
<Invulnerable>=RunningBack
<MusicBegin>=RedBlitz.wav
Wait <Touchdown>=RunningBack
<MusicTransition>=NextBar
Follow <MusicBegin>=RedBlitzTouchdown.wav
<End Script RedBlitz>
```

<Begin Script> and <End Script> are self-explanatory. Words in pointed brackets define the execution of game code. Words in square brackets define player input. Nonbracketed words are either objects or actions whether it's a running back in the game, a music file, or a command object like <NextBar> (which activates a particular kind of music transition).

This all makes sense, but is it really that user friendly? Not really, especially for those who aren't already familiar with all the syntax I've had to describe. Imagine scripting like this using Visio and you'll have a much easier time translating the English into the code (**Figure 8.7**). Some development teams are already incorporating this kind of compilation system, and having a GUI on the integration end will be a great help for the staff member who integrates the audio into the game.

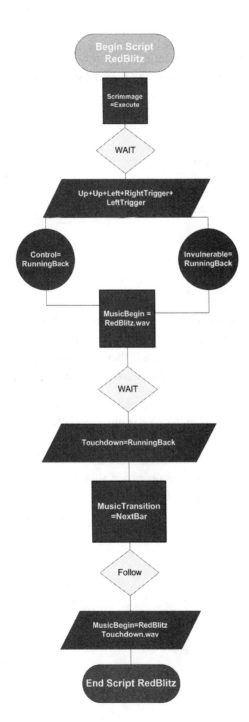

FIGURE 8.7 We've used Visio for our DPMs; now we can use it to visually describe a scripted event.

Voice-over Integration

Voice-over is different from everything else we have attempted. Today's games can have more than 50,000 lines of dialogue. With this many assets, organization is extremely important to ensure that the characters speak the correct lines.

Fortunately, the complexity of voice-over integration lies only in the large number of files. The system for playing the files themselves is fairly straightforward: Start by using an internal tool that looks at the game's script where the lines of each character are stored. When the line is triggered, this tool searches for the correct line and plays back the voice file.

What's important for the audio professional is to know how the files should be named. With 50,000 files, using unique and descriptive filenames is foolhardy. Therefore, use numbers or a combination of letters and numbers. Often a programmer will generate these letters and numbers randomly, then write code that recognizes the randomly generated filenames and associates them with the proper lines. When the system I mentioned searches in the script for the correct line, it looks up the right filename even though it might appear meaningless to an audio integrator.

But wait, suppose a line that was already recorded and named needs to be edited? No problem. The same code that generated the filenames and associated them with the lines will spit out the correct filename when the line in question is entered into this tool. The audio integrator can then easily look up the file, edit it, and save it.

Proper File Formats for Porting

I've left a surprise for you at the end of our integration fun. Before you begin creating any assets at all, you should be aware that different platforms have different file-type requirements. I left this bit until the end just so that I could ensure you'd read the whole chapter and wouldn't be put off by these technical requirements at the outset. (I know, pretty sneaky of me.)

Begin by creating all your files in the highest-quality format you think is appropriate. Today the average high-quality format is 44.1 kHz, 16-bit WAV. By the time this book is published the file format may be 96 kHz, 24-bit WAV. Regardless, *always* make your files using this format to start with. Whether you need to edit files or convert files for another platform, the file always sounds better if you down-sample it (convert to a lower bit rate or frequency range) from a high-quality format rather than start with a lower-quality format and save it again. Saving a lower-quality file after editing it, especially after you've changed its volume, always degrades sound since data can be lost with a volume change.

Once you have a master directory structure with all your high-quality files organized in it, it's time to convert the files into the proper formats so they can be played back on the platform for which you're developing. Suppose you're developing audio simultaneously for the Xbox and the PlayStation 2. The Xbox uses a proprietary ADPCM (adaptive differential pulse code modulation) format, called Xbox ADPCM, as does the PlayStation 2, called VAG. Both WAV and VAG files have a 4:1 ratio to the original file, meaning a 40 Kbyte WAV file will be 10 Kbytes when converted to ADPCM or VAG. But when you convert a WAV file from its original high-quality format, it can develop artifacts that manifest themselves as a very slight crackle depending on which frequencies are used in the sound. High frequencies usually are subject to artifacts more than low ones are.

If we convert our Xbox ADPCMs to PlayStation 2 VAG files immediately, the very slight crackle becomes an even bigger crackle. But if we convert the original files into both Xbox and PlayStation 2 ADPCM formats first (at the same time), both have the slight crackle and neither suffers much.

Delivery Systems: What Do People Really Want?

In this chapter, we have explored advanced audio integration techniques that generate better game audio—but keep in mind these techniques don't rely on any particular technological advancement. They are simply development techniques that let you explore your creativity within a game environment.

When developing audio technology, it's easy to get wrapped up in what we as developers think is important and ignore the simpler perspective of the average game player. Let's take two big features in game-audio technology that have worked their way into the latest and greatest titles and rationalize their importance based on a more careful examination of our market.

Surround Sound: Convenience or Nuisance?

Surround sound began appearing in games in the early to mid-1990s. Dolby Laboratories, one of the world's leading audio companies, began to take an interest in games around that time, earlier than most household-name companies (such as Technicolor and MGM Studios) did, in fact. However, at the time, Dolby was asking developers to integrate surround sound into its games. I was one of those developers. When I asked how this could be done, the reply was, "You can add it to your movies, but we don't have a way to do it in real time just yet, while the player is actually in the game itself." This wasn't a very satisfactory answer. While Dolby had good intentions, it was exploring a development market it didn't yet understand.

Now, the Dolby logo appears on nearly every game released, especially those for the Xbox and the PlayStation 2. I have a very good relationship with the company, but I still ask myself how surround sound benefits a game and how it enhances the experience.

In 1998 the game *Aliens vs. Predator* was being shown at the Game Developers Conference, at a booth for Creative Labs. This company, now called Creative, entered the game industry building sound cards and now produces just about every audio device imaginable. In this conference display, the company was showing off surround speaker systems.

The setup consisted of two front satellite speakers (3- to 4-inch-cube speakers that provide sound similar to that of a larger speaker when used with a separate subwoofer) and two rear satellite speakers. I thought *What the hell*, and stepped up to the exhibit.

Aliens vs. Predator, a first-person game, had a distinct advantage because it used sound effects from the movie *Aliens*. The use of these sound effects in conjunction with the surround sound was startling and very effective. I felt as though I were a space marine about to be eaten—and not in the same way that companies advertised pixelated graphics and claimed "astoundingly realistic graphics!" in their advertisements. The graphics weren't what made it real—it was the sound.

The many games that now use a 3D first-person perspective benefit greatly from surround sound. Since the player's perspective is the same as that of the character he is controlling, sounds that come from behind the character can also come from behind the live player. Flight simulators and driving games—any game that puts the player in the position of controlling the character's action from his own perspective—benefit from surround.

For games that aren't designed with a first-person perspective, surround is not as important. It can serve to make things sound cooler, but not more realistic. And because all games, whether 3D first-person or not, are still presented on a 2D surface (a monitor or television), sound that encompasses the player is a leap beyond current display technology. Until games become holographic in nature, it will remain that way.

What about the market? Do people really want to worry about arranging speakers behind them in the middle of their living room to achieve surround sound? It's clearly not easy to make surround speakers ergonomic. When my last house was built, I installed spaces to accommodate surround-sound speakers, but I never hooked them up. My point? Call me old-fashioned, but I didn't need surround sound. What is everyone else doing? According to Dolby, more than 100 million surround-sound systems are in use in homes across the United States. This doesn't speak for Europe or the rest of the world, but it suggests that a large portion of game players have surround-sound setups.

The verdict is therefore in: Surround sound for first-person perspective games helps, and there's a market for it. For other kinds of games it is less effective, but that doesn't mean it can't be used.

Qualitative Study: 22 kHz vs. 44 kHz

Audiophiles in studios across the country are clamoring for higher digital quality for recording and playing back sound. At the moment, 192 kHz 24-bit sound is the highest possible quality that can be distributed in a portable format (DVD). The majority of games still use 22 kHz 16-bit sound, however.

The reason 22 kHz is still the standard for games is that even though it is not the quality people expect on a music CD, it is good enough. However, 20 sound effects played at 22 kHz sound worse than 20 sound effects at 44 kHz. In some games, sounds with a large range of frequencies may use 44 kHz for those on the high (treble) end, and for bass-heavy sounds, a frequency range of 11 kHz can work. Some people have even suggested that a game seems to *look* better when higher-quality sounds are used.

It has been found that 192 kHz yields additional frequency overtones that weren't accounted for in the original postulates about 44 kHz. Taking this a step further, let's ask this question: Does this mean we should try to use 192 kHz sampling? The answer is simple: Of course we should! Just because people accept something of lesser quality and it's effective "enough" doesn't mean we shouldn't strive for better quality. People accepted the quality of grooved cylinders for gramophones ages ago, but they wouldn't accept it now. It's up to game-audio developers around the world to continue raising the bar.

9
Looking Ahead

WE HAVE SEEN how knowing a thing or two about process can help you work more efficiently on a project. We have also looked at more creative ways to produce and integrate audio so that the people playing our games have more fun. Now it's time to consider future possibilities in game audio: Specifically, how can we make audio development processes and methods even better?

Ideal Approaches

When someone complains about their job, often the complaint comes from an ongoing or repeating aspect of the job that the person doesn't like. It could be because the task is mundane. Or maybe the task was inappropriately assigned to the person in the first place. My father taught me that when you face a situation like this as a manager, you should ask the worker, "If you could picture an ideal situation with your work, what would it be?" In game audio, a composer may wish to fix a problem in a particular piece of music, but the real problem could lie in the composer's role on the game team, or the actual process of creating music for the game. Focusing on the problem in that piece of music doesn't get at the deeper problem. Is the composer's job of writing music as easy as it could possibly be? No? Then instead of focusing on the piece, let's reevaluate the entire process, even if we're only brainstorming. This is the ideal place to start for reworking a process to make it more effective in all aspects. In this chapter I will present a number of ideal approaches for game-audio issues and plan for the future.

The Popularity of Game Audio

From day one, game-audio folks have complained about not being recognized for their outstanding efforts, by their peers and the public. Let's start by asking whether this is important, then look at the ideal approach to this issue.

Why should game-audio folks be given awards? For one thing, creating good game audio is very difficult. It isn't as important as developing a new kind of heart medicine or solving the overpopulation problem, but it's hard compared with plugging instruments into amps in a garage and jamming away. The musicians who jam so well, and are so highly regarded that hundreds of thousands or even millions of people buy their music, deserve recognition. The same applies to game-audio developers. Many do it, but few do it well. The ones who are considered top-notch deserve to be recognized. By "best" game audio, I mean that which game-audio professionals as well as the public consider unique, memorable, and effective; the sound and music of the movie *Star Wars* fall into this category.

What would be the ideal way for game-audio developers to get the proper official recognition? An unrecognizable logo that looks like an award on one's Web site isn't necessarily the answer. Game-audio development is a very specialized and difficult skill to master, whether you're talking about directing the audio, composing music, directing voice, doing sound effects, or programming the audio. Any of the skills associated with game audio are just as respectable as they are in film. Thus, recognition is warranted for people who create the titles that are most successful in the eyes of their colleagues as well as the public. If there was a game that deserved such distinction in audio, it would be the award-winning *Thief* series.

In an ideal world, game audio would be categorized according to its specialty for both developers and the public at large. A number of groups—including the National Academy of Recording Arts and Sciences (NARAS), which also runs the Grammy Awards—do this with music genres. The Academy of Interactive Arts and Sciences (AIAS) promotes outstanding production values in games with its awards each year. AIAS gives out various awards for games but does not specialize in game audio; instead it gives awards for all aspects of games. In 2004, for example, its categories for game audio included best licensed soundtrack, best original music composition, and best sound design. The only group that has a set of awards tailored to all aspects of audio for games is the Game Audio Network Guild (GANG).

For any particular award, anyone can submit music titles and games that have outstanding audio in the appropriate category. A number of organizations already accommodate this, including AIAS and, more specifically for audio, GANG.

Ideally, this is how the awards would be decided: Each year, any person who wishes to register may cast a vote by phone, on the Web, or through the mail. The sponsoring organization (GANG, AIAS) tallies the votes, and awards are given out accordingly in a ceremony that is broadcast on national television.

How close are we to this scenario? Except for the national television broadcast and the ability for anyone to vote, we're already there.

The question that remains is why game-audio awards shows aren't broadcast on national TV. The answer is simple: Nearly everyone knows what a movie is. Not nearly as many people know what a videogame is. Yes, that's correct; film and television still have a majority when it comes to familiarity, not to mention popularity. While I don't have figures to confirm this, most people older than 60 may know what a videogame is but aren't familiar with any current games. Ask anyone you know who's that age. The same group will be familiar with current films or television shows.

If you take a look at the U.S. Census Bureau figures for 2001, you'll see that 105 million homes in the United States had at least one television. Worldwide in 2003, videogame-related sales reached $5.8 billion, which includes 232 million consoles sold. Because an unknown percentage of households have more than one console and we're comparing U.S. figures with worldwide figures as well, these numbers would imply that significantly fewer households have game consoles. The number is growing steadily, however—20 years ago, only a few hundred thousand households worldwide had game consoles.

While it's true that significantly fewer homes in the United States have consoles than televisions, we can estimate that approximately 40 million households do have them (extrapolating from a 2001 count, according to Alexander and Associates, of 35 million).

A demographic of 40 million makes national coverage worth arguing for. More and more awards shows (SAG, the Golden Globes, the Emmys) are being broadcast nationally. However, the issues and rules concerning what is broadcast are in the jurisdiction of the big TV networks' programming coordinators. A nationally syndicated "pay" network called G4 focuses exclusively on games, but its viewership is far smaller than, say, NBC's.

At this point it's easy to see how videogame audio would be excluded from what's considered mainstream. After all, nationally syndicated commercial networks get their money from, well, the commercials. The vast majority of products sold on the major networks via advertisements are mainstream products that everyone uses. Videogames are advertised on commercial networks, but not videogame audio specifically. Most of the products have something to do with cars, food, or clothing: things that most everyone uses. According to U.S. Census Bureau estimates for 2003, more than 290 million people live in the United

States. Most of those people are driving around, eating, and wearing clothes. When the number of people playing videogames grows to at least half of that number, it'll be a good bet that videogame soundtracks and videogame audio as a whole will be a more viable subject to feature on commercial television.

Now that we've discussed the popularity of game audio in an ideal world, let's explore it in reality. Numerous fan sites on the Web are devoted to promoting game soundtracks; I'm sure a search on Google for "game music" will yield those that are currently the most popular. Here are two excellent resources:

Music4Games (`www.music4games.net`)—This site focuses on all current game music. It is not a historic site but features the latest and greatest achievements by game-music composers, film composers doing game music, and pop star licensees.

GameMusic.com (`www.gamemusic.com`)—Oriented primarily toward Japanese game-soundtrack releases, this site sells many good soundtracks, mostly imported. It also has a Top 40 section and a reviews area in which readers may post their thoughts on soundtracks.

Popularity Challenges

Some people regard game audio with very little respect, for several reasons. First of all, game audio is currently being compared to audio in film and television in terms of dramatic effect and production quality, but for the most part it has not yet reached the standards of film in that regard. Some game-audio developers are addressing this issue by incorporating orchestras, famous choirs, and pop acts into their game soundtracks. Are these the only ways to attain a par with film and television? Hardly. They are the easiest and most obvious ways. Better composition, more interactive and adaptive composition, and an ear toward more elaborate mixing and engineering will eventually prove more effective for original audio and licensed soundtracks alike.

Second, most producers and team leads take voice acting less seriously than they do soundtracks. They invest less time and money than would be necessary to yield something competitive with film and television, and game voices therefore do not sound always convincing or realistic. This is a nearly universal problem with games, and it's another reason the sound quality of games isn't as good as that of films.

Finally, game audio has a tendency to have annoyingly repetitive sounds because of hardware or software limitations (such as RAM or storage space). For example, it might seem like you hear the same footstep sound a million times before you finish a game. It's perhaps one of the greatest threats to game-audio quality, whether in voice, music, or sound effects.

Ideal Game Audio

No doubt about it, game audio has come a long way from the bleeps and bloops of the primitive audio synthesis in early titles. However, we still have a long way to go. To see how we can take game audio to the next level, I will now paint an ideal picture for all games, and then establish parameters of audio perfection for each game genre. If these ideals can be achieved, game audio will certainly be given more respect. Let this be my final word before I sign off.

All Videogames

Ideally, game audio will be addressed at the beginning of preproduction. The publisher or developer will hire an audio director or manager to oversee all audio production during the entire project. This director or manager will know how to consider the game's design and technology to create a budget and schedule that address the game's audio production and integration needs.

Game-audio tasks will be specialized into appropriate fields. Game composers would not create sound effects, for example, and game producers would not direct voice actors. Here's an ideal staff roster for any game project's audio:

- ▶ Audio director
- ▶ Composer
- ▶ Sound designer
- ▶ Sound engineer

More than one specialist can be hired (freelance) or assigned (in-house) based on the work that needs to be done, and the specialists don't have to be present for the entire project.

Games will not repeat audio unless a musical theme is being restated. In that case, the theme will be varied each time it is restated (known in compositional terminology as *theme and variation*).

Conversations between characters will be paced properly and voice acting will sound realistic. The player won't have to push a button to hear the next line. Conversations can be replayed but not delayed.

Game soundtracks will feature music that is appropriate for the theme of the title. In driving, fighting, and puzzle games, the player can choose the music. Licensed music should be considered carefully. Using an already released single isn't as good an idea as using an unreleased song or remix, because a game can serve as a song's launchpad just as easily as the radio can. Game audio gains much more credibility when it gets the first shot at a song release, and game players have something much more interesting to associate with the song than having flipped on their boom box.

Ideally, game soundtracks will be interactive and adaptive: Based on player actions, they will change in some way. This is what will differentiate games from linear media such as film and television.

Fighting Games

Fighting games in particular will benefit from nonrepetition. Injury sounds should number in the dozens if not hundreds to ensure a variety of effects. *Soul Calibur 2* achieves this through the use of many attack, hit, and reaction sounds at random.

While it's usually better when a game's music is free of lyrics, fighting and driving games are the exceptions. These are probably the most appropriate types of games to use voices. Both genres have a singular focus and singular goal, so lyrics would not be distracting during gameplay.

FIGURE 9.1 *Soul Calibur 2* continues the tradition of Namco's ability to create a magnificent fighting game.

Again, music will be adaptive. According to changes occurring during a fight or because of a special move, the music could change and thus increase the player's satisfaction.

Driving Games

Adaptive soundtracks have already been used with some success in such driving games as *Need for Speed 3: Hot Pursuit.* When a police car approaches, the music changes to be a bit more nerve-racking and tension-filled. This is a good example to follow. The same can be done with licensed soundtracks, and the results are effective. In the same way that various soundtracks within a song (bass, guitar, drums) are unmuted when the player captures the right amount of "globes" (spheres) in the game *Frequency,* the music can change when the player passes other cars and reaches checkpoints in a driving game. Each trigger can activate or deactivate a particular music track.

Some driving games give the player complete control over the music that is played, just as one would with their own vehicle's sound system or radio. The first examples of this were Sega's *Out Run* and *Out Run 2,* which allowed the player to twist a dial at the start of the game to choose any song they liked (from a fairly narrow selection).

FIGURE 9.2 Sega's *Out Run 2.* In the original *Out Run,* players could use an onscreen radio to select the music they wanted to listen to during the game.

Sound for car engines has improved by leaps and bounds. Now many different sounds are used to generate a very realistic-sounding engine in videogame racing cars. The ideal is a combination of real sounds and synthesis to generate a dead ringer for the genuine article, in much the same way that Guy Whitmore suggested for adaptive audio in Chapter 4, "Design."

Puzzle Games

Guy Whitmore set a new standard for adaptive soundtracks in his music for such games as *Russian Squares* for the Windows XP Puzzle Pack (see **Figure 9.3**). Other puzzle games can use this model, whether with custom music or licensed music.

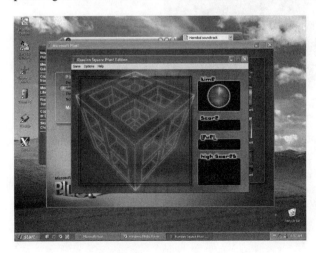

FIGURE 9.3 *Russian Squares* uses a complex sequence of music segments to achieve a great adaptive score.

Some games, such as *Pikmin,* have a soundtrack whose tempo quickens as the difficulty increases. Even with this adaptive feature, sounds in puzzle games can be terribly repetitive. Understandably, especially in a puzzle game, abstract sounds (such as single-toned beeps and unique sounds like *whirr*) are vital for player feedback and to identify events when they can't be designated any other way. However, if a sound must be used over and over again, vary it a bit. As long as the basic sound is still there, you can create a much better experience for the player.

Sports Games

Each sport has a set of defined rules, which you can use to create an adaptive soundtrack. For example, when a team makes a score, music can play until the next segment of the game begins, thus making the transitions between segments seamless. Music can also come from the PA system in the game world itself, to add to the realism (many sports games, including Electronic Arts' *Madden NFL,* already do this, but not in conjunction with the game's soundtrack).

FIGURE 9.4 Electronic Arts has been setting standards in football videogames since releasing the first *Madden NFL* in 1991.

Since crowds are a staple of sports, a sports game should have an entire system devoted to the sound of a crowd and its reactions to players' actions. This crowd sound should be properly mixed with the music.

For hockey games, it's now technologically possible to create a realistic sound system for the sound of skates on a hockey rink.

Action/Adventure Games

This is a broad category, but fortunately most action/adventure titles use the first-person perspective, which lends itself to specific techniques for audio.

All games in this genre will take ambient sound into consideration. Any kind of environment has sound of some sort, unless it's a fantasy environment in which you don't want environmental sound. Just as textures paint a visual landscape, sound helps paint a sonic landscape for the player. In fact, sound "textures" are starting to be applied to visual textures in the game editing environment. In *Half Life 2* (**Figure 9.5**), textures play an important role in how objects sound when they collide with each other. When you have multiple objects moving (such as car tires or a rock slide), it's critical to take these sounds into account when creating an overall ambience.

FIGURE 9.5 *Half Life 2* was one of the most highly anticipated action/adventure games of 2004, mostly because of its extremely high-quality graphics, mature science fiction–based plot, and textured sound effects.

Surround sound will be a staple of three-dimensional first-person games, as action/adventure is the ideal game genre in which to use this technology.

The Future

What can we expect to see in game-audio development in the coming years? I decided to ask three high-ranking, seasoned game-audio industry professionals their thoughts on the future of game audio. Their responses follow.

Interview: Guy Whitmore

Guy Whitmore is the technical editor of this book for good reason: He has executed some of the most advanced techniques in adaptive audio for recent games across multiple genres. Not even the ex-LucasArts audio team could boast that, as all of its games were graphic adventures.

AB: *What do you think the largest advancement in game audio will be in the next five years?*

GW: I would like to think that a big advance in adaptive music will happen, and I'm sure such steps will be taken. However, it may be closer to ten years before highly adaptive scores become a wide reality. There are three limiting factors, or hurdles, that I see before us.

First, composers must be willing and excited to take on the huge challenges of actually scoring a game. Currently most game composers don't score games as much as they create music to fit the general moods of a game. That has to change if significant advances are to be made in adaptive music for games.

Next, there is a complete vacuum of tools for creating adaptive scores— particularly tools that are available to the public. Composers are forced to reinvent the wheel each game, even to gain very basic adaptive features for their game.

Last, the industry, namely publishers, must be convinced that highly immersive game scores are a positive trend, and that it will make gamers more excited about spending money on their games. Currently the focus has been on overall audio fidelity, and that's a great thing, but I believe that trend has temporarily cooled publisher interest in more adaptive scores.

In the next five years the most significant audio advance will likely come in the area of advanced mixing of SFX. There's already a keen interest in getting game SFX as intense and powerful as in blockbuster movies, but there's more to it than simply making great individual sounds. The current limiting factor for SFX is how they're mixed in the game.

CONTINUED ▶

Interview: Guy Whitmore, continued...

I believe we'll see more real-time intelligent mixing in games. Tools like Xact for the Xbox and Scream for the PS2 are leading the way and will make huge leaps in the coming years.

AB: *How do you see licensed music working in games compared with movies and television?*

GW: Licensed music is already a fact of life in games, and I'm sure the trend will continue to mature. As with movies, there will be good artistic use of licensed content, and there will be examples of blatant abuse of it by marketing departments; for example, "What is this Eminem song doing in my kid's alphabet learning game?" Differences in how the game industry uses licensed content may appear in coming years when gamers get tired of linear songs being stuffed into their interactive environment. Special licensing deals may be made to create adaptive versions of pop songs, such as in the game *Frequency*, so that they may be an integral part of the gaming experience. Currently, licensed music is simply aural wallpaper in games.

AB: *What is the ideal sound setup you can imagine for games, whether it exists now or whether it could be built in the future?*

GW: Well, let's go to fantasyland: Start with surround outputs from the game machine being converted with Apogee converters and played through Genelec speakers. Make sure the room is a theatrical space at least 15 feet by 15 feet.

Perhaps the surround sound could add an "above" speaker and a "below" speaker. That would make dogfights and helicopters more intense. May as well go with 24-bit, 96 kHz sound, since fantasyland has no memory or processor constraints. The real-time DSP (digital signal processor) would be on a par with the best Lexicon and TC Electronic algorithms. The adaptive score would be accessing a GigaStudio-type sampler and the finest software synths, all mixed in real time. Ah, just a few short years away...

Interview: Tommy Tallarico

One of the best-known game composers in the industry is Tommy Tallarico. His company, Tommy Tallarico Studios, has developed audio for more than 200 games. Tommy also wrote some excellent old-school soundtracks including those for *Earthworm Jim* and *Cool Spot*.

In addition to all that, Tommy is the founder and president of the Game Audio Network Guild, the game-audio industry's largest professional organization. He also hosts two television shows devoted to videogames: *Judgment Day* and *The Electric Playground*.

AB: *What do you think the largest advancement in game audio will be in the next five years?*

TT: On the music side I think you'll see the production quality go way up. More people will start to use live musicians and orchestras. More composers from film and television will start to cross over as our budgets get bigger, and people will start to mix and master their music professionally as opposed to doing it in their own studios. 5.1 surround-sound mixing will become very popular, and the use of more in-depth, powerful streaming will allow for all of this live music to be implemented in a more interactive way.

I also believe that as story lines and game plots get more compelling, you will see us moving away from creating music based around what "level" you're on or what the "environment" is, and more toward motifs centered and triggered around the characters. Because of all of this, you will see a lot more videogame soundtracks hitting the market as well.

From a technical standpoint you'll see a huge jump in the audio tools available to sound designers and composers that allow them to infinitely control the sounds in an environment. This will take more of the integration element away from the programmers and put more of it into the audio designers' hands, where it belongs.

CONTINUED ▶

Interview: Tommy Tallarico, continued...

AB: *How do you see licensed music working in games compared with movies and television?*

TT: I think it will work in exactly the same way, and I think we are already seeing that now. As in films, some artists will be contracted to create an original song, and some popular music will be licensed for certain scenes, cinematics, or levels. Just like the movies, games can have the original soundtrack and licensed music work well in certain areas. Some games, like *Halo,* will never need licensed music—similar to, say, a *Star Wars* movie. Yet some games, like popular sports and driving titles, will only need licensed music. Both kinds of games can coexist happily just as they do in film and television.

AB: *What is the ideal sound setup you can imagine for games, whether it exists now or whether it could be built in the future?*

TT: The gaming experience is all about 5.1 right now and in the future! Consumers are making videogames the center of their home theaters. Systems like the Xbox and the PS2 support digital audio output for true 5.1 sound. Once you've experienced a game like *Halo* in 5.1, there's no going back! A great subwoofer is key to a 5.1 videogame experience. Motion pictures sometimes use back channels and the sub for certain explosions, pass-bys, et cetera, whereas in videogames 5.1 helps engulf you entirely into the experience and is constantly being used when traveling around a 3D environment.

Interview: George Alistair Sanger

George Alistair Sanger, aka The Fat Man, and his Team Fat company have been responsible for a good deal of some of the most cinematic-sounding games in the '90s, including *7th Guest* and *Wing Commander*. The latter title in particular was the first game that players described as "feeling like a movie," which was a rare feat in that era of games.

George has written music for more than 300 titles, and he wrote a book on game audio that I highly recommend: *The Fat Man on Game Audio: Tasty Morsels of Sonic Goodness.*

AB: *What do you think the largest advancement in game audio will be in the next five years?*

GS: The thing that most needs to be overcome is the repetitive nature of game audio. Basically the problem can be seen as a mathematical one: A game will play for 40 hours. What game company in history has had the foresight or the wherewithal to set aside enough budget, disk space, and attention to make 40 hours of interesting audio?

Although some hold great hope for algorithmic audio engines, I see these as Band-Aid fixes that are at best helpful for only some situations. An "autocomposing" program or even a clever "variations engine" may be capable of filling a hotel with wallpaper, but not a museum with art. My experience tells me that there is a direct correlation between the amount of care a composer spends on audio and the artistry of what results.

This leads me to believe that there might be two ways in which the problem of repetition might be approached over the next five years. The first approach would allow the composer to put more artful care into the audio. That would likely happen when we finally get nonproprietary cross-platform authoring tools—tools that will allow a composer to control how his linear sounds sit in the interactive context of the game. Such tools will be massively useful and really start leveraging off each other when they can speak to a common file format, the way MIDI-enabled tools can speak to MIDI files.

CONTINUED ▶

Interview: George Alistair Sanger, continued...

The second approach to solving that [repetition] problem would likely involve a radical rethinking of the relationship between sound designer, sound file, game, time, intellectual property, and such. In other words, rather than responding to the need for more work and more care from the composer, one might examine the problem with an eye on distributing audio more efficiently.

I would look at a model in which the rich library of sounds and music that have already been created for published games and then lost in the ether of game history are reused from game to game. They then are carefully channeled and filtered so that they give precisely the desired auditory effect in a given game situation. As an alternative, I would suggest that a game *not* use a specific sound or even a pool of sounds for a given event, but rather produce audio by tuning in to a specific Web- or disk-based *radio station* with a very narrow stylistic range.

AB: *How do you see licensed music working in games compared with movies and television?*

GS: Why, I think the use of licensed music in games is just super, just like in movies and television.

Except that it's a likely sign that the game's developer is so totally insecure about his own ability to be an entertainer that he has hired another [failing] industry to act as entertainer for him, in hopes of having better odds at "safer" sales numbers.

And except that people who buy games have come to distrust any licensing as a cheapening and selling-out of the value of the game in favor of associations with famous people.

And except that the very "safeness" behind that decision betrays the fact that the game is probably based on a mentality of "playing it safe to please the investors" that runs exactly opposite to the risk-taking aesthetics that underlie all of [game development] itself.

CONTINUED ▶

Interview: George Alistair Sanger, continued...

And except that it squanders the budget and disk space on audio that will become sickeningly repetitive the very second it repeats.

Other than that and a bunch of other things, it's super!

AB: *What is the ideal sound setup you can imagine for games, whether it exists now or whether it could be built in the future?*

GS: Stereo is fine. The attention given to all this technology is inappropriate to the return on investment. Surround is nice. Bass is overrated but OK. More speakers is better but quickly becomes expensive and extravagant.

You know, a little force feedback, some stereo or surround, and you're just fine. Today's "ultimate" system is ultimate enough for five years from now. If your system is accurate enough to make you think somebody's in the same room with you, and that's not hard to achieve, then you're at or near the level of sound system that [anybody] can appreciate.

I would encourage all gamers to take that extra $100 a year that they might spend on "ultimate" sound systems and write a letter to their favorite game company. The letter should offer that company $25 if they will put $75 into composing ten seconds more original music for the game. I think that would be a great sound system!

As you can see, there's a lot of room for game audio to grow, but there's also a great deal to be learned from the past with the work that has been done.

If we consider all the work that modern game audio entails, we can take advantage of the concepts we have learned using our development process maps. And by keeping an eye on the constantly evolving technology and design principles, we can create a truly amazing media experience in which the user controls not just the sights they see, but the sounds they hear as well. We can develop and integrate our audio in such a way that every decision leads to a genuinely impressive audio response.

Index